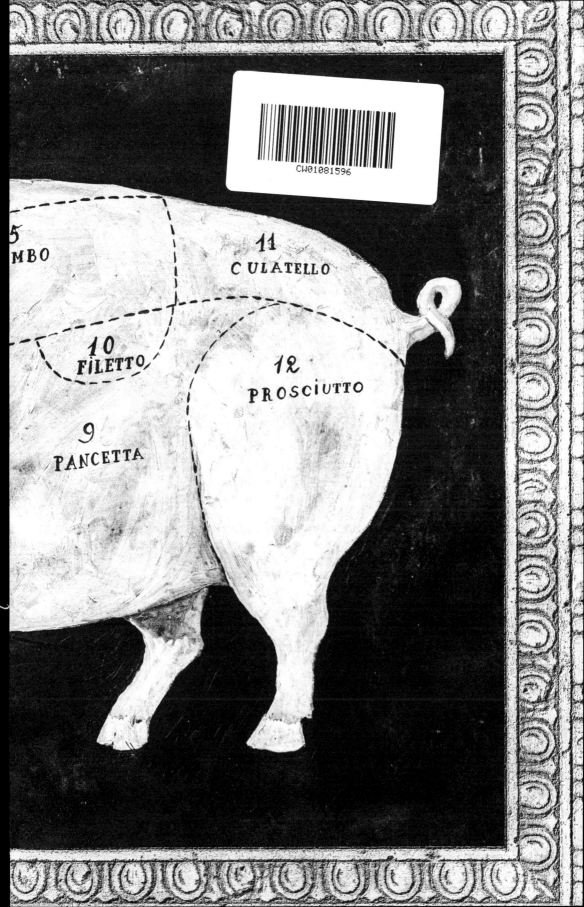

NEVER WELL-DONE

Tales and recipes from Farm to Fork
Toscana

40 recipes by Stefano Bencistà Falorni

SİMEBOOKS

Monteriggioni, herd of roe deer crossing the frozen countryside near Abbadia Isola.

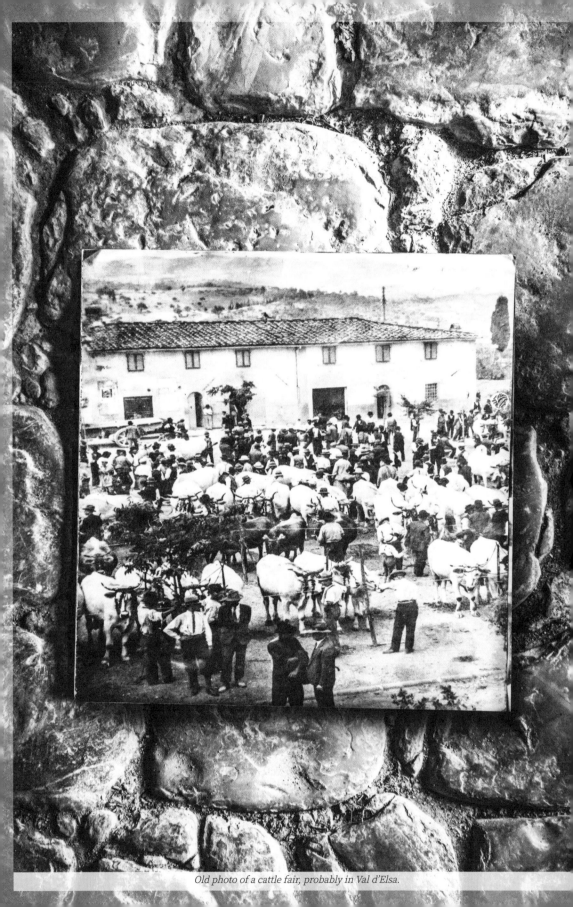

Old photo of a cattle fair, probably in Val d'Elsa.

Dear Reader,

This is a book about Tuscany. But not about its landscape, cypresses and olive groves, cities of art and medieval villages. It's about meat, meat cookery and the culture of meat cookery. In Tuscany. It is a distinctive feature of this region that it sets such a high value and quality on this particular food and at the same time is capable of treating it with common sense. That's is why it seems right to explore the subject.

Take the Tuscan excellences in this field, for instance. There are so many that it would have been impossible to deal with all of them in these short pages, and we apologize for having left out along the way more names and stories than we have been able to include. No one should feel excluded. We are dealing here with an immense world, and we have tried to recount a piece of it with which everyone can somehow identify themselves.
But what interested us most of all was to express a concept of sustainability and culture. The two things go together and a subject as delicate as everyday food, which has to be in harmony with respect for animal welfare and the fragility of the environment, needs an advanced laboratory to understand how to evolve in a balanced way. Here it is. In the Tuscan rural tradition we found a trace, an idea of that laboratory. The idea is that perhaps – probably – if we breed animals in harmony with nature, if we respect the cycle of the seasons, if we use the land better, if we eat less meat, perhaps we will save ourselves. And we will live even better.

Apart from saving ourselves, we will save the lives of those animals that we have sacrificed for millennia for our own subsistence, we will save an ethic of life and protect it from the logic of arid, blind profit. We will also save an idea of beauty, because where there is respect for nature and harmony, there is beauty. The same beauty that we find in every fold of the hills, in the stones and bricks that shape villages and cities, in the fields of olive trees and in the rows of cypresses that often mark that complex equation of historical, anthropic and natural factors that are accustomed to call "landscape". So now we have returned to the same clichés and are once again praising the Tuscan landscape ... But it is inevitable: everything is part of the whole, and behind a quality ham or a memorable steak, there can be nothing but a world of harmony, there can only be beauty.

In this book you will also find some recipes: they are simple, satisfying, easy to make. Try to interpret them, make them your own. This is the most sincere invitation we can offer you. Rather like sitting down to table in Tuscany.

Bon voyage. And enjoy!

Tuscany

Summary

Trattoria La Casalinga, Florence, wine and menus.

List of recipes

Landscape near Buonconvento.

Why a book about meat?

You have to be crazy, I won't do it. What am I going to I tell them? What will I say when the frightening numbers are waved under my nose? The numbers that record the consumption of land, water, the lives of those poor creatures doomed to end up in pieces on a supermarket counter? You have to be crazy to write a book about meat cookery in a historical moment when if you chomp on a steak a crowd will point at you as the world's number one enemy.... You must be crazy. I won't go around Tuscany talking to these cow and wild boar killers to justify their primal instincts. Make a book out of it? You must crazy, I won't. But I want to understand it better, because it's impossible for nourishment – a fundamental activity in human history – to be an opinion and so it is, rightly, questionable. The real madness –truly unforgivable – is not understanding things.

Let's start with the numbers, the ones that are scary.

30% of the land under cultivation worldwide produces fodder to raise livestock for slaughter. The world population numbers some eight billion individuals, but quantities of food are produced every year that would be enough to feed twelve billion. And despite this one billion people continue to have a very limited access to food resources. Put simply, many inhabitants of planet Earth suffer from hunger and are malnourished, while another large percentage eats too much and badly, this time to excess.

A Tuscany that smells of salt, grass, rain-soaked earth, smoke from ovens and chimneys.

And the livestock? Raised in batteries, locked in cages without being able to move, stuffed with artificial food, hormones and antibiotics. Their sacrifice, even before reaching the slaughterhouse, is not death but life. So? Why should we keep talking about meat as a food for people?

Greve in Chianti, Piazza Matteotti. The heart of the town. People throng the porticoes, shops and stalls on a market day. In the piazza there is a monument to Giovanni da Verrazzano, a navigator and explorer who dwelt in a castle in these parts and from here he set off in 1506, at just twenty years old, to make landfall in Normandy and then cross the

Stefano Bencistà Falorni with a rib of veal.

Aging cheek at the Falorni butchery.

Atlantic Ocean three times. Giovanni meticulously explored the eastern coast of those wild lands that would later become the Americas, a name given in honor of another Florentine navigator, Amerigo Vespucci, who in the same years sailed the routes of exploration with those of the young man from Verrazzano. How two Florentines – who had only seen the waters of the Arno – become great navigators remains a mystery, but that's another story. Anyway, the monument is here, and behind the monument, there is a historic butchery, the Macelleria Falorni. The scent of prosciutto and pepper carries a long way. Framed in a setting of gigantic old chopping boards and stuffed wild boars, here is a shop crammed with meat, meat in all its forms and interpretations: cured meats, loins, ribs, sausages, ox quarters and steaks. Prosciutti hanging from ceiling beams, showcases with all kinds of knives and tools of the trade, and then pieces of lard camouflaged with rosemary, skewers loaded with meat ready for grilling and slices of every sliceable kind of salume. A shrine of its kind. It is in this setting that Stefano Bencistà Falorni comes to meet us.

Falorni is a Tuscan macellaio or butcher. He has always been a butcher, also an explorer, in his own way. It must be a freak of these people, never being able to stand still. His house and shop are in the piazza of Greve, from where – another mystery – you get a clear vision of the world.
Born in 1947, since childhood he has been a macellaio (general butcher) and norcino (pork butcher) traveling from farm to farm. Stefano has lived through extraordinary years of peasant culture, he has known the splendor and misery of this civilization, always between the street and the shop, from house to house, meeting people, slaughtering animals, working and celebrating, inventing, struggling to keep going and make alive and resilient a history that otherwise would have been lost. An explorer in his own way, we said: on foot and within his world.

This is the man who will accompany us as we get to know a piece of Tuscan culture. A Tuscany that smells of salt, grass, rain-soaked earth, smoke from ovens and chimneys. The land that saw the birth of humanism and has always kept the virtuous balance between history and nature, cannot fail to teach us something even when it comes to food and animals.

Eat less, eat better is Falorni's first piece of advice. To make known the origins of things is the purpose of this book, because today more than ever we are what we eat.

Rotisserie in my style

Technique: *meat cooked on the rotisserie*

Time: *3 hours 40 minutes.*

Ingredients: *sausage, bread, pork, chicken, liver, small game birds, lamb, bay leaf, sage, rosemary, salt, pepper, 2 slices rigatino, 4 veal chops, breadcrumbs, hog caul fat, liver.*

First of all, light the fire in the fireplace and the barbecue.

Prepare the small game birds by cleaning them and adding salt, pepper and sage.

Spread out the chops and lay the rigatino cut into strips on them, roll up and tie carefully.

Chop the sage, rosemary and bay leaves, cut the liver into small pieces (postage stamp size) and mix well together, adding a little breadcrumb. Tie into small balls with the caul fat.

Cut the pork, lamb and sausage into regular pieces.

Cut a frusta (long narrow loaf of bread) into regular slices.

Season with salt and pepper all the pieces of meat and begin to thread on the spit a piece of chicken, bread, pork, bread, sausage, bread, liver, bread, game bird, bread, lamb, bread … and so on until the spit is full. Remember to add sage to each piece and rosemary for the lamb.

Make sure the fire is hot and embers abundant, then turn on the rotisserie over a low heat for 3 hours.

In praise of poverty

If you want to know the meaning of a word, you could look it up in a book – a dictionary – which will give you the answer. Inevitably you then tend to get lost amid all its wealth of words, but precisely in this lies its beauty and also its usefulness. Because getting lost in the pages of a dictionary as you search the alphabet for the right word is a marvel of discovery, of worlds hidden behind other words.

Nowadays we do a search online. It is quicker and less adventurous, but we lose a lot of nuances, which in the meanings of words are as important as the substance. They are themselves substance. Let's take an example: *povertà* and *miseria* online are said to be synonyms. But that's not true. The Romans distinguished between *miser, inops, pauper,* three different degrees of poverty, and even in Italian one difference remains: *povertà* is lack of money, *miseria* is also connected with happiness. On the negative side, of course: the *poveri* are just poor, the *miseri* are poor and wretched. And so a large part of humanity has lived miserable and unhappy. Then there are the rich.

Palaces, works of art, thoroughbred horses, crystal, sailing ships, silverware, hard cash, gemstones, watches, telescopes and violins, alabaster statues... The list of beautiful things that wealth has inspired and produced appears endless, and much of our artistic heritage would not be so in the absence of past patrons. But if we accumulate riches just because they are made of gold and glisten, their value vanishes on a horizon of spectacular banality. Wealth is ultimately boring when it produces more wealth and feeds only itself.

The poveri are just poor, the miseri are poor and unhappy. Then there are the rich.

Fortunately, wealth can also be different, more interesting: liberation, a state of grace, the need for few things, invention. In short, a relative, minimalist wealth, the only authentic kind and the only kind worth striving for. All poverty tends towards wealth by starting from the *miseria* it opposes.

And the *miseria* to be opposed was measured, down to the 1950s, especially in the kitchen. No other parameters existed: the possession of things – the things themselves – were reduced to the essentials and the real difference was between those who had something to eat every day and those who did not. The path to follow was struggle, search, a continuous battle to survive and to make the taste for life survive. In this way, the evolution of cooking took place, in Tuscany perhaps more than elsewhere. The need to find something every single day to put in the pot and on the table to feed the family.

The tales of miseria and the ways people managed to find something to eat are very moving. Listen to this, for example. The tanners of Santa Croce sull'Arno used to scrape the last shreds of fat from the skins boiled with blood and dust to make a dish called *cioncia*, a kind of stew of fat, cooked with onions, celery, carrots. Without a similar reason – the goad of hunger – there would not be so many good things to eat today: *finocchiona, ribollita, peposo, lardo di Colonnata, lampredotto....* Ultimately almost everything that was once poor today is traditional Tuscan cuisine.

So give heartfelt thanks to those brilliant and unfortunate generations that transformed their personal *miseria* into a steaming pot of food. They were not cooks so much as alchemists, inventors, in some way thaumaturges, and into the pot they threw – together with their souls – the little they had. Then they sat down to the table thanking the Eternal Father (in those days that was the custom), they ate and got up. Still poor but no longer *miseri*, no longer wretched.

Sign of an old butcher's shop in via di Beccheria, Siena.

Leaves of parsley, Petroselinum crispum.

Land

Food. We have to start with food, cibo in Italian. And its meaning. One of the probable origins of the Latin word cibus is the Greek term kabos which seems to have meant a measure of food, the quantity it takes to feed a man for one day.

Crops were cultivated and harvested, with a verb for each type of harvest: reaping, picking, mowing.

This is food. In this definition there is already an ethical measure of the relationship between man and nature. This measure, based on the peasant social organization and on the structure of farms, those places where food was produced until a few decades ago, arrived intact from the Middle Ages to the 1960s, when the power of industry changed the place of many things, the course of many lives. Cities become metropolises, the countryside was depopulated and families scattered. Food lost its primary meaning and became a consumer product, an industrial product. The peasants became workers and citizens.

Not that the peasant's was an easy life. The work was hard and poverty left no hope of redemption. You were born a peasant, you died a peasant. But you always found something to eat. The peasant did not go hungry. His diet was vegetarian because the only products that abounded were those from the field and the garden. Historians say that in northern Europe they called us "leaf eaters" and it was not a question of trend. In our countryside every day many people had to sit down to table because the land was worked with hands and families had to be big. Long tables and they ate meat, if they were lucky, once a week.

Around the house lay the land. Between the house and the land there were the things needed to feed the community, for small-scale buying and selling, for the maintenance and construction of useful things. The vegetable patch first of all, with potatoes, pumpkins, zucchini, onions, lettuce, tomatoes, and then trees: pear, apple, cherry, plum. A well for water. If possible, a thicket would be left intact. It meant having firewood, kindling for the oven, animals for game, mushrooms, berries and roots. And wood for making tool handles. Willows would be planted along the sides of fields, with their shoots being excellent for tying up vines and weaving baskets, frails and panniers. Somewhere there would always be a mulberry tree, for the silk trade that had its greatest expansion in the Medici period, when traders went from house to house collecting the cocoons and paying for them in cash.

And then above all there were always animals. In the barnyard there were hens, turkeys, ducks; farm animals: rabbits, pigs, pigeons, sheep, or work animals such as oxen, cows, donkeys; domestic animals like cats and dogs that kept away the mice, foxes and stone martens. There were also wolves, which eventually disappeared and are now making a comeback.

Finally the land. Whether it was a lot or a little, three things were grown on it: wheat for flour, olives for oil, grapes for wine. They tilled and harvested, combining a verb for each type of crop: reap, pick, harvest.

Then the wheat would be taken to the mill, the olives to the press, the grapes to the winery. In exchange, they obtained flour, olive oil and wine. Hardly ever money. That began to arrive when they realized that, instead of using oxen, the plow or the cart could also be pulled by cows. They were not so strong, but in return they gave birth to a calf each year. The calf could be sold and brought in some money. Then came tractors, but by then the real peasants had already left the land.

In this context, the domestic economy was fragile, the only certainty was that food, cibo, would never be lacking. Bread and wine were sacred, meat – when they had it – was precious. The peasant ate the first chicken of the year for the festival of the Three Marys, in mid-August, and it was always a great celebration.

We have to return to loving the land, the animals, the things we eat.

Traditional farmhouse in the countryside of San Casciano, Val di Pesa.

The Beccai

Orsanmichele is a giant stone cube, resting in the heart of Florence as if it had landed there coming from another planet. They have tried to refine it with statues and triple lancet windows, but basically it remains a square stone block. This is the impression it gives from the outside.

Seen from inside, the ground floor of the building is a richly decorated church. You don't get it at first because the architecture is atypical, the ceiling is low, the decoration is sumptuous, but then you see the altar and you realize you are in a church. Beautiful too. On the first floor there is a museum. It has the same architecture as the floor below but lighter and brighter, higher and with an exhibition of statues to justify the name. Nice too, though. Going further up there is a large empty space where you finally see what Orsanmichele was meant to be and never was: the city's granary. And then you suddenly understand the austere architecture of the building: a box. Orsanmichele was a stone box with wheat inside. And around the box there was a whole circle of traders, bankers, artisans. Florence, a mercantile city inclined to sober pragmatism, had gathered around its granary the guilds, known as the Major and Minor Arts, so that they could meet, do business and enable the city to prosper. It was the guilds that transformed the ground floor of the granary into a church, so as to fulfill their commercial duties and religious observances without wasting too much time.

At 4 via Orsanmichele, in the shadow of the largest and richest Palazzo dell'Arte della Lana, is the palace that from 1318 to 1534 was the seat of the guild of the Beccai, the butchers, or rather of the guild that brought together butchers, fishmongers and tavern-keepers.

In 1593 Ferdinand I ordered that the shops on the bridge be freed from the "vile arts".

The butchers weren't very polished people. Their guild became large, rich and powerful, so much so that it also conquered positions in the city government, but it never won the approval of the Signoria or city government. The prejudice had a long history behind it.

According to tradition, the first "evil and cursed butcher" in history was Cain. The rest was done by the butchers themselves: unwilling to compromise, aggressive and quarrelsome, perhaps even inclined to cheating on a small scale. Their work was subjected to very restrictive rules enforced with a firm hand, especially the obvious rules concerning sanitation or the obligation that the meat should come from authorized slaughterhouses. Prices were restricted, weights and measures controlled. Despite this, according to the chronicles of the time, corruption was widespread and the unreliability of the butchers as a class was proverbial: "the promises of butchers are like the bladders of their animals filled with wind" was a saying that alluded to the common stratagem of inflating carcasses to make them look bigger.

These weren't just petty commercial offenses. In Florence as in Siena, many of these carnaiuoli were also cattle merchants and so economically even more powerful. At various times the guilds became involved in palace intrigues or real revolts, without ever having a successful outcome. They were the first to be forced to adapt to each new urban development. In Siena the butchers were moved from their old premises at Fontebranda to the "comfortably adapted shops" of via di Beccheria, while in Florence over the centuries the butchers were even more nomadic. In 1318 we find them in Ognissanti and the Mercato Vecchio, in 1442 at Ponte Vecchio, until their most famous eviction by Ferdinand I. In 1593 he ordered that the shops on the bridge be freed from the "vile arts" and the butchers, fishmongers and greengrocers were moved back to the "Mercato Vecchio" (now Piazza della Repubblica), to be replaced by goldsmiths and jewelers.

Even their fellow tradesmen, the tavern keepers, were under the control of the authorities. If they served pies of meat, roast spleen, fried liver, fish and roast birds to criminals, thieves or women of easy virtue, the guards of the Signoria would arrive and order fines, whippings and even the destruction of their premises.

Pizzicagnoli, norcini and macellai

The chubby one is a talker, the little one a loner, the third has a quick eye. It sounds like a Western, and so it is, to some extent, being a story of blood and knives. There are three men in this story: the pizzicagnolo, the norcino and the beccai. And it's not going to be a shoot-out but an eat-out.

These are not things you learn in school. To understand them you have to walk over tons of manure.

The talker is the pizzicagnolo. He is someone who has a delicatessen where he sells food. To be more precise he sells delicacies and the finer the food he sells, the better the pizzicagnolo. I was forgetting to mention that this curious name comes from the verb pizzicare, meaning to be sharp or rather pungent. Many of the things he has in his shop are pungent, being prepared with salt and spices. You can also smell the odor about him, on the white apron smeared on his basically rotund profile: he has the physique du role and is dedicated to his occupation. He is a central character in the life of a Tuscan town. He could easily be the mayor of the town, if only he wanted to change his daytime job. He does not lack authority and popularity. Through his shop pass the finest things that the community produces and here they are discussed and judged: salumi (cured meats), hams, cheeses, bread, olive oil, wine. He will also sell some basic necessities for the home and in the most extreme cases some agricultural tools. Sometimes, rarely, the pizzicagnolo will produce on his own some cured meat or ham and whenever he does, it is sure to be outstanding. In most cases he visits the producers, chooses, selects, tastes, buys, takes them to the shop and sells them. This is why he chats easily. He has to communicate.

The solitary and taciturn one is the norcino or pork butcher. It seems that the best ones once came from Norcia (in Umbria), hence the name and a certain reserve. The pork butcher is ultimately from Umbria. People call the norcino to houses where they still raise pigs today. He brings his tools, fixes everything and kills the hog (the verb used is amazzare, not uccidere or one of its many synonyms). Then it is boned, the cut for making prosciutto is removed, and the rest is turned into salami, insaccati, salsicce. In short: the hog is transformed from a living creature into a multitude of products which, once seasoned, are ready to eat. But the norcino doesn't have time to stop and chat. Once his work is finished, he sets off along other roads to other houses, other pigs. A killer. The fact is that the hog is killed in a limited period of the year, between just before Christmas to shortly after Epiphany (6 January) and all the year's work is concentrated into those two weeks of cold and festivities. And everyone wants the norcino, not because he is a ruthless killer, but because butchering a hog is an art, and he – taciturn and solitary – is the artist.

The macellaio or general butcher has a quick eye. He is a curator of meat, he knows all the different kinds of livestock – sheep, pigs, goats, cattle, poultry and game – and how to breed them, cross them, hunt them. He knows the kitchen and knows what the cook needs to prepare the various dishes. The macellaio occupies a middle world, he accompanies the animal from the farm to the kitchen. The butcher has a quick eye because his great ability is to "see" the animal. If you don't "see" him, if you can't judge its breed, weight, origin, age, state of health at a glance, you will never be a good butcher. It's something you don't learn at school, to understand it you have to walk over tons of manure.

"Better to smell of hog than smell of poverty." It is in the cattle sheds that the trade is handed down from father to son. And this is history. The reality today, a little less poetic, is that every butcher carefully chooses his cattle breeders and trusts them. But beware of trying to outwit him. The butcher has a quick eye.

> *"In via dell'Agnolo*
> *there's a pizzicagnolo*
> *who had a pimple*
> *on his little dimple"*

(says the old Florentine nursery rhyme)

Roberto Falai, norcino in Val d'Elsa.

Butcher's tools, Falorni Collection.

The butcher's tools

1 - ACCIAIOLO (STEEL)
for sharpening knives

17 - CASTRINO (CASTRATING KNIFE)
for chickens

2 - SGORBIA (GOUGE)
for deboning the ham

16 - SARRACCO (SAW)
for butchers

3 - SBOTTATOIO (TROCAR)
for sheep and cattle carcasses that swell during hanging

15 - COLTELLO (KNIFE)
for deboning

4 - RADDRIZZASEGHE (SAW STRAIGHTENER)
to adjust the teeth of the saw or sarracco

14 - COLTELLO (KNIFE)
for pigs

13 - BLADE
to skin pigs

5 - PINZA (STICKING PIN)
for killing pigs until the end of 1968

12 - CASTRINO (CASTRATING IRON)
for pigs

11 - PINZA (PLIERS)
for lead seals

6 - ANNOCCATOIO (SPINAL CORD CUTTER)
short dagger for cutting the spinal cord of cattle until 1960

10 - COLTELLA (KNIFE)
to cut the hip bone from prosciutto

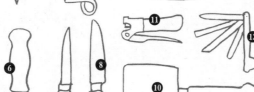

7 - COLTELLO (KNIFE)
boning knife

8 - COLTELLO (KNIFE)
for choosing meat

9 - COLTELLO (KNIFE)
with a broad blade for skinning pigs

Roast chicken and rabbit

Technique: *pan cooking.*

Time: *1 hour 30 minutes.*

Ingredients: *half chicken, half rabbit, sage, olive oil, thyme, lemon, salt, pepper, white wine.*

Cut both the chicken and the rabbit into 6 pieces, put them in a large pan together with the olive oil, sage and pepper and brown the meat on high heat.

When the meat is browned, add a glass of white wine and let it evaporate.

Continue cooking over medium heat for about 1 hour, add the lemon juice, stir constantly and finish like this until it is well roasted.

Fritto dell'aia prepared by Paolo Bacciotti, Trattoria da Tullio in Montebeni.

Fried chicken and rabbit

Technique: pan frying.

Time: 1 hour.

Ingredients: half deboned chicken, half deboned rabbit, flour, 2 eggs, salt, rosemary, lemon, sage, extra virgin olive oil.

Marinate the chicken and rabbit cut into bite-sized pieces with the lemon juice and salt.

After flouring the chicken and rabbit pieces, roll them in a mixture of sage, rosemary and then in the beaten egg.

Fry them in boiling olive oil and serve in a straw paper bag.

Chicken and Co.

Livorno, a port city, has a shrine on the top of a hill formerly surrounded by a dense forest, hence called Montenero, from which the sanctuary takes its name. It was on that hill, "5 miles southeast of Livorno", a center of pilgrimage for sailors who had survived storms, fishermen who had received a miracle and fearful seamen that, in 1852, a local young peasant couple went to ask Our Lady to intercede to ensure a peaceful journey, to calm the sea and give them a warm welcome on the other side of the Atlantic. The two were about to emigrate to America, with little money, 27 Leghorn hens, a rooster and a lot of hope. Carrying chickens and roosters seemed like a good idea, because there weren't any in the New World at that time. The trip went well, the rest is history. Today in the United States almost 60 kilos of chicken are consumed per person per year, which means raising nearly 7 billion chickens. We like to think that they are all descendants of those 27 hens and that rooster which left Livorno that day many years ago.

The two were about to migrate to America, with little money, 27 Leghorn hens, a rooster and a lot of hope.

More than three centuries earlier, however, the Spaniards had imported turkeys from the New World. Creatures of the wild, undemanding and easy to breed. They produced a large amount of fine meat. The turkey passed from hand to hand, spread rapidly throughout Europe and here, in Tuscany, a small breed arrived, called the lucio, which shared the barnyard with other fowls. Hens were kept only for laying eggs. They brought in just a little money, but it was reliable. Some chickens were allowed to grow up and become hens to lay eggs or be eaten (farmers would eat their first chicken at mid-August). The finest chicks were then allowed to grow into roosters, the less fine ones became broilers and finally the least fortunate became capons just before Christmas. I talked about all this to Angelo "Giangio" Zani, 91, whose family has lived on the same farm for six centuries. I asked him to tell me how many animals there were at home when he was young.

There were a lot of turkeys, as many as 20 or 30 each year. The farmer would sell nearly all of them, keeping only a few for himself. One they would eat at All Saints, another for

Pollo Valdarno Nero, bred by Laura Peri, Montevarchi.

Carnival and the luckiest ones were kept to renew the breed. There were 40 to 45 hens and two roosters. Turkeys plus chickens: 60/75 animals around the house.

Then there were the paperi or young geese, bred all over Italy since ancient times – just think of the Capitoline geese. Not to be confused with ducks, which in Tuscany are called nane and roam quietly around the farmhouse, and all the better if there is a pool of water. There might be a dozen geese, the ducks even more numerous – as many as thirty – but never as numerous as the pigeons that in Tuscan houses had a privileged home in the dovecotes. These were turrets set at the center of the building, in the roof, where the pigeons loved to nest and could be easily caught. Colonies of sixty, seventy pigeons were frequent. In all that makes some 180 animals around and above the house. Then, inside the house, protected by the walls of the stable, there were rabbits. In a cage, quiet, prolific, there would be lots of them, even more than thirty. Less numerous but bigger were the oxen. Sturdily built, they were used in working the fields, but they were later replaced by cows, which were not so strong, but could have calves, and the calves could be sold to a butcher, as was also done with the pigs. The peasant, if he could, would raise a good number of them to sell or slaughter for himself. The hog was called the "farmer's moneybox" because it was easy to raise, brought in money and gave him meat.

By adding rabbits, cows and pigs to the account, you get to 230 animals, but we must not forget the sheep: about thirty in the best years. And that makes 260. And then some donkeys, of the Amiata breed, docile and useful for carrying weights, when everything was measured "by the hundredweight" and the donkeys carried bales, sacks and carboys as far as the main road on the ridge of the hill, 800 meters of laborious ascent. Horses came later. They would be the last of a community of 15 people and 270 animals.

Ask and you will see. Today hardly anyone knows what a chicken is. Laura Peri, who in addition to raising chickens, guinea fowls, ducks and pigeons explains to school children what these creatures are, has devised a simple but effective scheme. The chicken – pollo in Italian, from the Latin pullus, a young animal, is a specimen of Gallus gallus domesticus, which has not yet reached reproductive age. So a chicken can be either male or female but it's still a chicken. Only in the following phase can we distinguish between pullets and cockerels and then still further between roosters and hens. Just a matter of time.

And time is also one of the factors affecting the food quality of the chicken. The intensive farming of the food industry involves the slaughter of fast-growing broiler chickens when they are only 35 days old, while a native breed such as the Valdarno (black or white) raised in the open and feeding naturally is not killed until it is 150 days old. To make a good chicken, says Laura, it takes a forest and a lot of patience.

Better an egg today than a chicken tomorrow.

Diced chicken and potatoes

Technique: *roasting in a pan.*

Time: *50 minutes.*

Ingredients: *4 chicken thighs, a sprig of thyme, lemon, sage, potatoes, olive oil, salt.*

Skin the chicken and bone it (or have this done by the butcher), cut it into small cubes of 1 cm per side.

Peel the potatoes and dice them like the chicken.

In a nice large pan with plenty of olive oil, put the sage, thyme and chicken on the heat and brown well.

Add the potatoes, add salt and cook over medium heat for 30 minutes without leaving it, stirring constantly. When cooked it will be a nice hazelnut color.

Landscape near Monticchiello.

Chicken with rosemary and tomatoes

Technique: *cooking in a pan.*

****

Time: *1 hour 15 minutes.*

****

Ingredients: *1 free-range chicken, sage, rosemary, 2 cloves peeled garlic, olive oil, wine, 400 g peeled tomatoes, sprig of summer savory.*

****

Cut up the chicken into 12/14 pieces.

Put abundant olive oil (6/8 tablespoons), sage, rosemary, chopped garlic and the summer savory in a skillet or saucepan.

As soon as the herbs have wilted, add the chicken pieces and brown for 10 minutes. Add the wine and let it reduce over a high heat.

Add the tomatoes, add salt, pepper, cover the pan and simmer for about 50 minutes until the sauce is nice and thick.

In the kitchen at the historic Trattoria "La Casalinga", Florence.

Chicken with mushrooms

Technique: *pan cooking.*

Time: *45 minutes.*

Ingredients: *600 grams chicken, 300 grams field mushrooms, glass of white wine, olive oil, salt, 1 clove garlic.*

Clean the mushrooms and cut them into slices, cut the chicken into bite-sized pieces.

Heat the olive oil in a pan with the garlic clove.

Add the mushrooms, salt and cook them taking care to turn them often. When cooked, put them in a bowl.

In the same pan, brown the chicken pieces, turning them often. Deglaze with the white wine and cook as required (about twenty minutes).

When done, add the mushrooms and stir to mix everything together. Add salt and serve.

Chicken in a brick

Technique: *cooking on the grill in a brick.*

Time: *2 hours.*

Ingredients: *one chicken, sage, rosemary, lemon juice, salt.*

Butterfly the chicken and marinate it in lemon juice and olive oil.

Put the brick on the live embers, place the chicken on it, add sage and rosemary and cover with its earthenware lid previously heated on the embers.

While cooking, with a sprig of rosemary soaked in olive oil and lemon juice, keep the chicken moist and turn it from time to time.

When cooked, add sage, rosemary and salt to further flavor.

Vintage photo of the piazza at Greve in Chianti.

Chicken roulades with tomato and oregano

Technique: *pan cooking.*

Time: *1 hour.*

Ingredients: *8 slices of chicken breast (as equal in size as possible) 4 slices of rigatino, 2 cloves garlic, salt, pepper, tomato, oregano.*

Spread the slices, add salt and pepper, put half a slice of rigatino, roll up the slices and tie up.

In a pan put olive oil and minced garlic. Put on the heat and brown the meat well.

Add chopped tomatoes and a tablespoon of oregano, add salt and cook till done, adding olive oil or stock if it tends to dry out.

The same recipe can be made using veal slices.

Tuscan chicken liver croutons

Technique: *pan cooking.*

Time: *1 hour.*

Ingredients: *500g chicken livers, sage, half an onion, 2 knobs butter, 3 or 4 sage leaves, 1 spoonful capers, 3 anchovy fillets, white wine, vin santo, stock, olive oil, salt, pepper, 1 frusta (long narrow loaf) of bread.*

Wash the livers well, chop the onion and brown it in a pan with a little olive oil.

Add the sage and coarsely chopped livers, add salt and pepper and cook for 30 minutes, sprinkling occasionally with wine.

When cooked, pass everything through the vegetable mill using the disk with the large holes, adding the capers and anchovies, then put everything back into the pan and cook for another 10 minutes, moistening generously with the vin santo.

Cut the frusta into slices one finger thick, dip them on one side into the stock and spread the paste over them with a spoon or knife with a rounded blade.

Recipe for the vegetable stock

Ingredients: *tomato, celery, carrot, onion, parsley, basil.*

Time: *1 hour 30 minutes.*

Clean the vegetables and cut them into pieces.

Put everything in a large pot, cover and simmer for an hour and a half. Filter and add salt. The stock is ready and the boiled vegetables can be eaten separately.

In addition to the classic vegetables, you can add potatoes, zucchini and a bay leaf to taste.

Old panel with the cuts of a hog, Falorni family collection.

MBO

11
CULATELLO

10
FILETTO

12
PROSCIUTTO

9
PANCETTA

Pork

Of course man, of all creatures, is a strange beast. Many beautiful words, but zero gratitude. Take the hog, for example: if we have developed, it's thanks to the hog. If someone calculated how many pigs we have eaten in the last 2500 years, it would make a striking figure. Yet we find it hard to show gratitude to this animal: impure, dirty, we use its name as an insult. We never think of expressing our appreciation to it. Instead we should raise a monument to the hog. Fortunately, the people at Colonnata have done it for us. In the marble piazza, next to the inevitable plaque commemorating the anarchists, there is a monument to the hog. Small, a bit awkward, but it's there, and it expresses heartfelt gratitude.

In the beginning all pigs were black. That was the color and you had no choice in the matter. No one ever imagined that a hog could be pink. It was like imagining a green horse, so to speak. They were black. In Tuscany, even before it was Tuscany in the days of the Etruscans, there was the Cinta Senese, black with its lighter band. Then came the "Large White", a big pale English boar that overtook the Cinta, giving way to the "gray" or grayish marbled. A great big critter, in the Tuscan countryside it was known as the "farmer's moneybox." Instead of hoarding money or taking out bonds, people invested in acorns and fruit and made prosciutto and sausages. And it was "harvested" in winter, the season when the fields were resting. This is why the hog was so beloved.

In the beginning all pigs were black. That was the color and you had no choice in the matter.

After the invasion of the British "large whites" – giving rise to the Disneyan image of the pink hog – and the initial amazement at how much easier it was to breed these pale beasts, in Tuscany there was a return to favoring native or derived breeds. Raised free range, in line with a certain idea of tradition, healthier and after all, when the time comes for the hog to fulfil its destiny, a tastier and more delectable hog. Thanks to all pigs, thanks.

Pork fillet in jail

Technique: *roasting in the oven.*

Time: *45 minutes.*

Ingredients: *2 large pork fillets, bay leaves, rosemary, sage, salt, pepper, pork caul fat.*

Make a mixture of the herbs, cut the fillets into slices at least 4 centimeters thick and roll them well in the mixture with salt and pepper.

Once they are seasoned, wrap them neatly in the pork caul fat and put them in a pan in the oven with oil at 180°C for 30 minutes.

The caul fat in the oven will melt to reveal the ribbed pattern. Hence the name of the dish in Italian: "pork fillet in jail".

Old farm ledger.

Freshly cut and salted rigatino.

Pork liver in the style of Greve

Technique: *liver skewered and pan roasted in the oven.*

Time: *1 hour.*

Ingredients: *600/800g of pork liver, salt, pepper, breadcrumbs, sage leaves, bay leaves, a pinch of sugar and a pinch of wild fennel, 100g fresh pancetta, pork caul fat, 4 or 5 wooden skewers, olive oil.*

Wash the liver, dry it and place it on a cutting board together with the bacon cut into small pieces, with the sage, bay leaf, sugar, salt, pepper and fennel.

With a heavy knife or a mezzaluna knife, cut and mix until the liver and bacon are in small pieces.

Sprinkle with the breadcrumbs and mix. Use a spoon to make 4-5 cm balls and roll in the breadcrumbs to dry them.

Spread out the caul fat and wrap the livers in it. Thread 2-3 of them on each skewer, put them in a pan with a little olive oil and roast them in the oven at 180 degrees for 30 minutes.

hIC EST · DECEMBER

Allegory of the Months, Marchionne d'Arezzo, church of Santa Maria Assunta, Arezzo, 1216.

Pork neck with turnip greens

Technique: *cooking in saucepan and skillet.*

Time: *1 hour.*

Ingredients: *4 nice slices of pork neck, garlic, rosemary, salt, pepper, tomato sauce, turnip greens, a pinch of wild fennel seeds.*

First of all, boil the turnips in a saucepan in water and salt for 30 minutes (or buy them ready cooked).

In a big pan put plenty of olive oil and 2 whole peeled cloves of garlic and 2 sprigs of rosemary and fennel seeds.

Lightly brown the garlic, put the meat in a pan and half-cook it, turning it over and taking care to remove the garlic (to prevent it from burning). Cover the meat with tomato sauce, add salt and pepper and finish cooking for about 15 minutes.

Remove the meat from the pan with half the sauce, put the cooked turnip greens in the remaining sauce and stir well to season them. Serve the meat with its gravy and the turnip greens in the sauce.

Florentine roast pork loin

Technique: *roasting.*

Time: *2 hours.*

Ingredients: *1.2 kg of pork loin, salt, pepper, garlic, rosemary.*

Debone the pork loin, make deep incisions in it and sprig it with salt, pepper, leaflets of rosemary and pieces of garlic.

Spread over the pork loin a little more salt, pepper and 3 sliced garlic cloves, tie them up well and then tie the bone to it.

Put in a pan with a little olive oil and a glass of water and roast in the oven at 180°C for an hour and a half.

Slice finely and serve with its gravy.

Palazzo Pubblico, a Cinta Senese led on a leash.

Detail of the "Allegory of Good Government" by Ambrogio Lorenzetti, 1338/1339.

The Cinta Senese

Take a map of Tuscany and fold it in half horizontally, then vertically and then reopen it. At the intersection of the folds, more or less, you will see the region called the Montagnola Senese. It could be said to lie a little east of Siena, or north of Sovicille, south of Monteriggioni, but this would not convey the idea. The point to understand is that the Montagnola Senese is at the center of something called Tuscany.

Montagnola because it is more than a hill, yet not a mountain. Its highest peak reaches 671 meters. It is a karstic, wooded, gentle but at times impervious place. Rather than revealing, it conceals. An imperfect, rugged, hidden beauty.

Etruscan shepherds grazed their hogs here and called them together by blowing on a kind of whistle.

It was in these hills that the legend of Siena began and it is also here that the story of a rustic hog of a very ancient breed appears: the Cinta Senese. Celebrated by Ambrogio Lorenzetti in the fresco "Effects of Good and Bad Government" (1338/39 Siena, Palazzo Pubblico), the Cinta Senese was for centuries the only breed raised in Tuscany. For more than centuries, millennia. Etruscan shepherds grazed their hogs here and called them together by blowing a kind of whistle, and Romulus' soldiers ate these same hogs. Wild and not very prolific, it was risking extinction when in the 1940s it was crossed with the English Large White hog to produce the gray. A wild creature, shy, the Cinta has to be raised out of doors, in its natural woodland environment. This is because the Cinta Senese was the first breed of animal to be distinguished by a PDO (Protected Designation of Origin) and a rigorous set of rules has to be followed in raising it. Just three hogs can be bred per hectare, no more. To give you the idea, if you want to raise thirty you will need something like thirteen woodland soccer fields. The opposite of intensive farming. This is not all, since these hogs have the ancestral habit of digging up the ground looking for roots, tubers, truffles, and so, if you want to save the forest, you have to give the land a rest sometimes. You will have to move them on to another plot and rest the land until it recovers. It means that to raise some pigs you need to have a lot of land. It will also involve a lot of effort to keep up with the herd, take care of the litters, divide them by age, be careful they feed properly (food supplements cannot exceed 2% of live weight, the rest they have to forage for themselves). You have to take care of the wild soul of the Cinta, which is also beautiful, but in its own way: the first who tried to repopulate the breed were looking for a perfect model, with rigorous and replicable aesthetic canons. Seven generations later, when they realized that no two were alike, they surrendered to the stubborn, irregular beauty of this ancient animal.

All hogs are very good at finding truffles. They are no longer used for two reasons: they are not as selective as dogs and they dig holes all over the place to find any other tuber or root that attracts them. They are not as manageable as a dog. Leading an animal weighing 200 kilos on a leash could be a problem, and if it does find a truffle, who is going to take it out of its mouth?

During the winter, at 7 in the morning, Stefano Governi's Cinta Senese hogs are waiting for their daily ration

of food to supplement what they forage for in the woods.

Cinta sausage and beans

Technique: *pan cooking.*

Time: *1 hour, after preparing the beans.*

Ingredients: *300 grams of cannellini beans, 6/8 Cinta sausages, 2 cloves of garlic, olive oil, 1 onion, white wine, pepper, salt, rosemary.*

The main dish and side dish are prepared separately.

Beans:

Soak the cannellini beans for 12 hours, cook them in a pan with salted water over low heat. Remove them before they are fully cooked.

Put olive oil, crushed garlic cloves and sage in the pan. As soon as the garlic turns golden, add the chopped tomatoes. Cook for ten minutes before adding the cooked beans separately.

Add salt and pepper and mix carefully. Cook for 15 minutes and the beans are ready.

Sausages:

Meanwhile, peel an onion and chop it, put it in a pan with the olive oil and cook for 6 or 7 minutes over low heat, add the sausages and let it brown for a few minutes. Stir from time to time. Deglaze with the wine.

Add the rosemary and tomato, salt and pepper and cook over low heat for 35/40 minutes. At this point add the beans and continue cooking as required (not more than 15 minutes).

Salami, salsiccia

Here's my two cents' worth. The right choices arise from experience, and experience arises from the wrong choices. This is an example of the thousand platitudes that can be uttered about making the right choices, whether they are small or large. Not that the question should be underestimated, but in short, in the course of a lifetime when we are not given the right to choose the most important things (almost nothing of what is written in our IDs, for example), the doubt remains whether it makes sense to give so much weight to secondary choices.

Salami in the cellar, ham in the tower.

Here is a certainly secondary but important choice. Let's say you are a farmer and on a certain winter morning the butcher comes to kill your hog. Of course he doesn't turn up out of the blue. You called him, you chose the right time. The first thing he asks you is: what will we do? A question that seems vague, but is very precise. When you butcher a hog there are priorities. Prosciutto, for example. And then the shoulder, the ribs, all the lean part of the hog will be either salted down or become joints and be cooked. But all the pork fat has to be used in some way. And that's why sausages were invented: salami, sausage, finocchiona, just to stay in this part of the world. The problem is that there is a lot of fat and the lean is already earmarked to become what it should

be, No one would give up a prosciutto to make salami. So salami is made with the scraps from the other cuts. But that's not enough: on average two/three salamis can be made from the leftovers. Hence the butcher's question: if you want to get more salami you have to sacrifice something lean. Peasant philosophy: "There is no joy without suffering."

Today it is just a matter of taste, but once it was a matter of hunger. Making more salami meant making more use of the fat part of the hog. Generally a part of the shoulder is given up, the fat that is in the rear part of the hog, between the belly and the back, is used in fine grinding the rump of the hog and filled with squares of fat taken from the rump.

Technically, salami is a mix of ground lean meat, obtained by trimming the main cuts, and the pig fat. Further fat cut into squares is added to the mix.
Temperature and humidity play an essential role in ensuring it ages properly. We should

Finished dishes, sliced salami.

always remember that salami is pork that is eaten raw and perfect seasoning is essential. In the past, people made do with empirical techniques: the fire on the hearth, a bale of hay kept moist, the cold room and the warm room. Salami in the cellar, ham in the tower, to say that the salami is kept in the cold and the ham in the air. Cellars and towers, hay bales and abandoned rooms are a distant memory, but the role of temperature-controlled systems hasn't changed anything, it has only perfected an ancient process.

Salsiccia is made with a similar mixture, only a little coarser. This is a smaller sausage made to be eaten cooked. Generally salsiccia is not aged, but in some cases, taking great care, it can be seasoned for a short time, to make it a little drier and less greasy.

Mercato Centrale, Perini's spectacular delicatessen counter.

Finocchiona

The Milanese, what an effort! With them it's all hurry, hurry, hurry! When they decide to do something, you have a hard time keeping up with them. Some years back a guy came all the way from Milan to Florence after making up his mind to write a novel that would finally establish just how the Italian language should be written and in fact – this was about the mid-nineteenth century – the country really needed a common language. In fact, he then made a success of it.... In Chapter 11 of "The Betrothed" at a certain point Perpetua complains, "She finally realized that she had been fooled [infinocchiata in Italian] by Agnese." Infinocchiata. Now, why didn't he write raggirata or turlupinata, which is what they say in Milan?

No, Alessandro Manzoni, with the purpose of enriching his Italian to refine the novel that made him famous (and loathed by generations of students), came here to pillage words and idioms, drawing on the Tuscan lexicon and turning it into Italian.

Prosciutto, salami and sausages are made all over Italy, but finocchiona can only if made in Tuscany, excluding the islands.

And now we need to explain to everyone the meaning of the verb infinocchiare. It comes from the word for fennel, finocchio. The custom of putting wild fennel in foods that were no longer fresh or serving it to accompany a bad wine was widespread at the time, and infinocchiare gently alluded to this small, almost innocent scam. Moreover, the custom arose among the peasants. who used fennel to flavor dishes that were not very tasty, a custom that stemmed from the frequent experience of hunger and the eternal attempt to escape it. In practice, when a hog was butchered, once the salami and sausages were made, there was a large part of fat and some lean scraps that was not very good eating but it was a pity to throw it away. By mixing everything with wild fennel seeds, a sausage was made that could still be eaten, so saving the stomach and the conscience. Of course, pepper might equally have been used, but pepper was expensive, while fennel grew wild on the hillsides. They just had to go and pick it.

This is more or less the story, necessity made a virtue, the success story of a sausage. Today finocchiona is no longer a second best variety of sausage. It is still being made

Plate of salumi (cold cuts) at the Bar Divino, Badia a Passignano.

Sandwich with finocchiona.

because people like it and they have liked it – it should be said – for at least four hundred years The first documents recording the existence of this purely Tuscan salami date back to that time. It is also a distinction: ham, salami and sausages are made all over Italy, finocchiona is such only if made in Tuscany, excluding the islands. It must also be said that over the centuries the salami has been greatly refined and the use of spices in the current finocchiona serves to enhance its aroma and character, no longer to cover the flavors and vices of poor quality meat.

Since 2015 finocchiona has been protected by the IGP mark and consequently has to comply with a production specification that establishes in detail all the important points in its production: from the percentages of feed given to the hogs to the weight of the sausage, the consistency of the slices and the percentage of fat, the seasoning, aroma and flavor. In short, it is rather like inverting the meaning of history and giving a certainty, to those who eat finocchiona, that they will not be cheated.

Until a few years ago its popular name was sbriciolona ("crumbly") due to the tendency of the slice to fall apart when cut. It was also made in very large and particularly fat-rich forms. After obtaining the IGP mark, it can and must be distinguished: finocchiona is salami that strictly complies with the specification, sbriciolona does not. Nobody says it's better or worse: it's something else, bigger, fatter and it crumbles under the knife.

Prosciutto

What if modernity wasn't the cold wonder of technological devices, but the availability of truly useful things? Water, which arrives fresh or hot and clean in all our homes. Or salt, for example.

We know that a salt is a chemical compound and that there are eleven different types, including sodium chloride or table salt. It is a primary element, extremely common in nature, yet very precious. Salt has conditioned human life and changed landscapes and habits. In ancient Rome it was so precious that it was used as a currency and the only road that did not bear the name of an emperor was the Via Salaria, the road that brought salt to Rome and took its name from salt, like an emperor.

Making prosciutto is simple: you start with a hog raised properly, then it's just a matter of salt, time, wind and sun.

In the following centuries, the Salt Roads ran across the whole of Europe. In Tuscany the most widely traveled one stretched from Saline di Volterra, where there are important deposits or salt mines, to Valdelsa, crossed the Via Francigena and then branched off towards Florence, Arezzo, Emilia. A long and laborious history. Today, salt is available everywhere, all the time, like water. Do we want to talk again about what modernity is?

There were no refrigerators and apart from a little snow collected in winter and packed down in the cellars, the only way to preserve meat was to salt it, which is why it was so precious. Everything that not could be preserved at the moment was salted down. Subsequently, with electric energy and new techniques for keeping food, only what was too good to be eaten in any other way was preserved in salt. A leg of pork, meaning prosciutto.

Making prosciutto is simple. You just need to start from a hog raised properly, then it's simply a matter of salt, time, wind and sun. In short, nature. You start with the ham of a hog aged 10-11 months and weighing 170 kg. In this first phase the ham will weigh about 14 kg and only the cutting and trimming will be done in the butcher's shop, to remove everything that is not ham. Here one point should be noted. If there exist the optimal conditions (a dry, fresh atmosphere) for adequate curing, the producer will proceed with all the subsequent operations, otherwise the ham is taken "to nurse" at a ham factory, a specialized place which will follow the manufacturer's instructions to season it as instructed. There the first salting and the "massage" take place: the ham is salted, left to rest on horizontal boards and then massaged to loosen the muscle fiber and make it softer. This operation is repeated at least three times within twenty days, after which the ham will be hung for 120/150 days, during which the flesh will very slowly shed its moisture. Occasionally, with favorable climatic conditions – a north wind – the air will be changed in the seasoning room. This is followed by the toelettatura (or "grooming") and a first light kneading that is done with a paste of ground lard, rice flour (out of consideration for those allergic to gluten) and pepper. This paste is applied to the part of the ham not protected by the rind. Then it is aged for another three months, given a second kneading and another three months' seasoning. A year has passed since the first cut. The PDO specification requires a minimum aging of 12 months for Prosciutto Toscano, but for a quality product the period is much longer. To see if everything is going as it should, a check is carried out by tapping it, or else piercing the ham with a pointed tool made from horse bone to tell – by sniffing the pin when it's removed from the ham – whether it has any flaws or defects. After this examination and the third and last kneading and a further 5/6 months of seasoning, the ham is cleaned and put on sale. At that point it will weigh about 10 kg and be soft and tasty.

Prosciutto under the ashes, salami under the wheat.
Two goods were hoarded in every peasant house: wheat and ash. As World War II was drawing to a close, when the retreating Germans were plundering the livestock and all the edibles, the peasants who lived through that period recount that they tried to hide everything. The salami was stowed under a pile of wheat, the hams were hidden beneath the ash heap. After some time it was discovered that the cured meats were preserved perfectly and gained in aroma. So in peacetime the peasants continued to subject small numbers of hams to the ash and wheat treatment.

Stefano Bencistà Falorni's Prosciuttaia in the company's ham factory, where up to 1000 prosciutti are aged.

Lardo di Colonnata

Colonnata has a long life and an uncertain history. Emanuele Repetti in his *Dizionario Geografico della Toscana* published the first document written about Colonnata, the merest trace. "In the year 1570 the village numbered no more than 24 hearths" and in 1833 Repetti himself described Colonnata as situated "in the remotest part of the marble mountains of Carrara, from which town it lies 3 miles traveling to the northeast", then five kilometers traveling southeast and 500 meters higher. It was reached by a road that, even today, many people find hair-raising.

Yet it has been inhabited for a long time. If the archaeological remains tell the truth, "a long time" means at least from 40 BC. From that dates a statuette of Artemis, obviously made of marble, found near the town.

In those years, all we can say with certainty is that this region was the source of marble known all over the world, or what was the known world in those days: the Roman Empire, the Mediterranean basin. And there was also some competition. Greece, for example, produced a fine white marble, which was too expensive even for the wealthy Roman conquerors. So they began to dig in the Apuan Alps, taking advantage of the experience of the quarrymen of the Liguri Apuani, a people so rebellious that they had never submitted to the empire. But they were willing – so it seems – to train the slaves to work in the quarries. The first settlement to house slaves working in the marble quarries may have been Colonnata.

Now, all those people had to be given something to eat every day and there were no fields worth cultivating in Colonnata. You only need to glance down at it to see that Colonnata is perched on a mountainside, beautifully isolated amid glimpses of ravaged mountains and chestnut woods. You can't grow anything there, but you can raise pigs.
And of the hog, here as elsewhere, nothing was thrown away. But Colonnata went one step further, transforming an inedible part of the animal into a delicious salume.

The method is still the one used in antiquity. In marble basins kept in the cellars of the houses still called *grotte*, a layer of pork fat is laid down, taken from the hog's back and covered with rosemary, salt, garlic – as well as cinnamon, pepper, cloves, sage – and then again a layer of fat and then more salt and spices, until it reaches to the top of the basin. It is covered and left to age for a minimum of six months, during which a natural brine forms inside the basin which preserves the lard and cures it, making it very soft and tasty.

The Apuan Alps near Colonnata

A cheap and humble food, known to very few except for the quarry workers, Lardo di Colonnata recently risked coming to an inglorious end strangled by the European Union's red tape. Although it had been produced for centuries, its preparation failed to comply with the strict Community standards of hygiene and in Brussels at one time they said this was no longer the right way to make it. Humble and poor, but also rebellious, lardo has infected politicians and journalists with its anarchic soul. There was a lot of talk about niche products being threatened by the newborn European bureaucracy, and in the end a law was passed to save what had to be saved and what seemed like an evil turned out to be a benefit. Today in Colonnata there are 286 inhabitants and 13 *larderie* that annually produce a quantity of lard that is difficult to tell. In fact, I'm not going to. Long live lardo! Long live Colonnata!

Bruschetta with lardo di Colonnata

Technique: *grilled bruschetta.*

Time: *10 minutes.*

Ingredients: *bread, lardo di Colonnata.*

Cut the bread into regular slices about 1 centimeter thick and the lardo into thin slices.

Place the bread on the grill making sure it doesn't burn and turning it several times.

Before toasting the bread, place a few slices of lard on each slice and let it melt from the heat.

Deboned guinea fowl glazed with olives and capers with cabbage roulade, onion fondant and sage with anchovies.

Prepared by Chef Alessandro Della Tommasina, Enoteca Pinchiorri, Florence.

A brief history of hunting

"Seven pounds of saltpeter for the propellant, one of sulfur to fire it and eleven ounces of hazelnut or hemp charcoal as propellant. Melt 4 parts of lead and one of arsenic and drop it into cold water through a sieve of the appropriate size to make shot of the desired caliber "

At first people hunted with falcons, but that was when there were few people in the countryside and lots of game. Game was res nullius, it belonged to no one and so to everyone. Since Roman times it had been possible to hunt anything and everywhere. Woodland covered most of the region and nature – so it was believed – would always dominate human activities. The "seven pounds of saltpeter", the blunderbuss, the harquebus and the rifle arrived centuries later.

At first people hunted with falcons, but that was when there were few people in the countryside and lots of game.

Fifteenth century. A few generations after the Black Death, the cities were being repopulated and the countryside was returning to new life. The peasants at the time practiced subsistence hunting and a little trade, but the tradition of falconry was lost and firearms were rare and only used in war. People hunted game with snares, meaning traps made of nets, leghold traps, holes dug in the ground and sticky resins spread on the branches of the trees to catch small birds. This practice has left its mark in the region's landforms and place names. From that period date the stands of trees in the middle of the fields (the famous group of cypresses near San Quirico d'Orcia) and place names like Paretaio, Ragnaia, Bucine, places where game is no longer caught but the name has remained. In the small rural communities a common trap was called the diavolaccio. This was a sort of large upturned umbrella soaked in lime (mistletoe sap) and with a lantern in the middle. The hunt took place at night, the birds were attracted to the light and remained entangled and captured. Larger game was hunted with the asta, a sort of pointed spear.

Up to this time people used to hunt to eat, in the sense of surviving, especially in the winter months, when game was a fundamental supplement to the lean diet of the peasant. Game was no longer the Res Nullius it has been, but there was great toleration, or rather:

The Diavolaccio was used for catching birds.

there were no written laws. In 1549 Grand Duke Cosimo I thought he would change things and laid down some rules.

"No person of any degree, quality or condition may dare or presume in any way or for any question or on any pretext to hunt or cause to be hunted or hawked birds or game using dogs, nets, birds of prey or other instruments of any sort."

Cosimo also established the bandite, plots of land, mostly Grand Ducal property, in which hunting was allowed and regulated. One of the most spectacular was the Barco Reale, which extended around Villa Ferdinanda at Artimino and which included almost the whole of Montalbano and the neighboring plains. Only the Grand Duke and his guests could hunt inside that reserve of wild land (in those days there were also bears), bounded by a wall three meters high and thirty miles long.

In the early 1600s there were about fifty bandite in Tuscany and the laws that regulated hunting began to overlap and become complicated. In 1587 the first "gun license" and the first, rudimentary hunting calendar arrived. The following centuries saw regulations being issued with different approaches and practises to form that "monstrous and disjointed legislative mosaic" which Leopoldo II put an end to in 1856 with a law that remained in force until February 1923.

Then came modern hunting, which in the beginning was the hunting of the farmer: a man, a dog, a gun and the natural surroundings. More than hunting, it was a sampling, an exchange of attention and knowledge...

What came later, the reserves, the shotguns, the cartridges, the farmed pheasants, the indiscriminate shooting, trap shooting... it's not history, it's not hunting, it's not amusing.

Wild boar on the Montagnola Senese.

Stewed wild boar

Technique: *pan cooking.*

Time: *2 hours 45 minutes.*

Ingredients: *500 gr wild boar, garlic, bay leaf, rosemary, juniper, red wine, tomato sauce, olive oil, salt, pepper.*

In a pan, put the meat on the fire for 15 minutes so that it sweats and loses its gamey flavor.

Remove the meat and discard the liquid. Prepare abundant minced garlic, rosemary, bay leaf, juniper and fry it in plenty of oil.

Add the chopped wild boar over a bright flame, brown well on all sides, pour in 2 glasses of red wine and let it evaporate.

Add two generous glasses of tomato sauce, season with salt and pepper and continue cooking for 2 hours until the meat is tender and tasty.

The wild boar

A whole book would not be enough to tell how the boar and humanity, throughout history, have always been close, conditioning each other's existence. Of Eurasian and North African origin, the wild boar has always been a prolific, invasive and changeable animal. An inhabitant of all latitudes, extremely adaptable to the most diverse climates, it has been among man's favorite prey, though it has always resisted this by its extraordinary ability to hybridize and reproduce, which has given rise to one of the most varied animal taxonomies. The term wild boar (*Sus scrofa*) is applied to an animal that has almost seventy subspecies distributed over a large part of the planet.

Wild boar sauce

Technique: *cooking in the pan.*

Time: *2 hours 30 minutes.*

Ingredients: *400-500g wild boar, 2 ribs of celery, 1 carrot, 1 onion, a sprig of basil, oil, bay leaf, ground juniper, salt, pepper, red wine, tomato.*

Grind up the boar meat coarsely, finely chop the vegetables and put them in a pan with 4 tablespoons of olive oil. Sauté and add the wild boar.

Brown it turning constantly, add half a glass of wine and let it evaporate.

Season with salt and pepper and after 10/15 minutes add tomato and juniper. Continue cooking in the covered pan over low heat for at least 2 hours.

Benozzo Gozzoli, "The Journey of the Magi to Bethlehem", Palazzo Medici Riccardi, 1461, detail of a hunting scene.

Roast pheasant

Technique: *Oven roasting.*

Time: *1 hour 30 minutes.*

Ingredients: *1 pheasant, 10 slices of rigatino, sage, white wine, salt, pepper.*

Pluck and singe well, clean it and stuff it with small pieces of rigatino, sage, salt, pepper.

Salt on the outside and cover with rigatino. Tie it carefully so that the rigatino remains tied to it, put it in an oven pan and sprinkle with oil.

Roast at 180°C for 1 hour, turning it often and adding wine a couple of times. Once cooked, cut it into quarters and serve with the rigatino and the sauce.

The pheasant

According to Greek mythology, the pheasant was brought back by Jason, leader of the Argonauts, from the ancient region of Colchis by way of the River Phasis, now known as the Rioni, the main waterway of Georgia, which was probably a route for trade with the East. From the name of the river comes the common name of this bird of the order of the Galliformes.

In Europe it quickly spread thanks to a favorable habitat and a constant practice of breeding it that has continued from ancient times to the present. It is bred and hunted for its delicious meat, which has always been highly prized on every table.

Sweet and sour hare

Technique: *pan cooking.*

Time: *2 hours 30 minutes.*

Ingredients: *half a hare, celery, parsley, 1 onion, red wine, tomato, salt, pepper, black chocolate, vinegar, sugar, raisins and pine nuts.*

In a pan, cook the hare for 10 minutes without olive oil to sweat it and shed some of its gamey taste.

Remove the meat and discard the liquid.

Chop the vegetables well and brown them in the same pan with the meat with plenty of olive oil.

Add a glass of wine and reduce, add a good dose of tomato sauce, salt and pepper and continue cooking over low heat with the covered pan for two hours.

When almost cooked, add a good-sized square of flaked black chocolate and a nice sprinkle of red vinegar, a little sugar and raisins and plenty of pine nuts.

Cook for 10 minutes and serve with the rich, tasty gravy.

The hare

Extremely common throughout Europe and Central Asia, the hare (Lepus Europaeous) is known as a shy and meek rodent, whose defensive strategy is flight and mimicry. Lacking any means of offense, when attacked, the hare leaves its sett and runs at a speed that has become legendary (it can reach 70 km/hour). It runs with an irregular course, alternating straight stretches with great zigzagging leaps to bewilder its attacker and avoid leaving an unbroken scent. And the hare has many predators. In nature it is hunted because it is defenseless and by man for the delicacy of its flesh and the softness of its fur.

Wild boar on the Montagnola Senese.

Stuffed guinea fowl

Technique: *oven roasting.*

Time: *1 hour 45 minutes.*

Ingredients: *guinea fowl weighing 1½ kg, 4 slices rigatino, chopped sage, rosemary and garlic, 1 egg, 1 boiled potato, breadcrumbs and 300g of minced veal. Oil, salt, pepper.*

Debone the guinea fowl, mix together well the veal, potato, egg and a some breadcrumbs and make a small meatloaf, as tight and long as the guinea fowl.

Butterfly the guinea fowl, add salt and pepper, add the chopped herbs and the small meatloaf.

Roll up, cover with slices of rigatino and tie together well.

In an oven pan put plenty of oil and the guinea fowl. Roast in the oven at 180°C for a good hour. Turn off the oven and let it rest for at least 30 minutes, cut into thick slices and serve with its gravy.

Ristorante Le Scuderie, Badia a Passignano.

The guinea fowl

Anyone who has traveled to Africa, especially in the countries of the sub-Saharan region, will have noticed how common the numerous families of guinea fowl are. From these parts comes the guinea fowl (or helmeted guinea fowl, *Numida meleagris*). It was imported into Europe by the ancient Romans, who had a colony in Numidia, to raise them for the table. As a farmyard animal it has remained, often coming into conflict with the other barnyard fowls, whose habits it often imitates.

Duck in pork

Technique: *oven roasting.*

Time: *2 hours 20 minutes.*

Ingredients: *1.8 kilos of duck, salt, pepper, wild fennel, rosemary, garlic 7/8 slices of rigatino, vegetable or meat stock.*

Clean the duck, remove its internal fat, cut off the tips of the wings and singe the small remaining feathers well. Wash it well, stuff the inside with rosemary and 4/5 cloves of unpeeled garlic, fennel seeds, salt and pepper.

Cover it with rigatino and tie it well, put it in the oven in a pan with plenty of oil at 170°C and cook slowly, adding stock and turning it 3/4 times for about two hours.

Before serving, cut it into 8 pieces.

For the stock see page 62.

Duck sauce

Technique: *pan cooking.*

_____

Time: *2 hours.*

_____

Ingredients: *1 duck of about 1.6 kg, salt, pepper, 2 ribs celery, 1 onion, 1 carrot, basil, tomato, red wine, olive oil.*

_____

Clean the duck, remove the fat, singe the duck and divide it into six pieces.

Finely chop the vegetables and put them in the pan with half a glass of oil.

Fry the vegetables, add the pieces of duck and brown well. Pour in some wine and deglaze.

Season with salt and pepper, add the tomato and cook for 1 hour.

Remove the pieces from the pan, remove the skin, bone them with your hands, fray the meat, put it back into the pan and cook for another 15 minutes.

Use the gravy as sauce for pasta.

Preparation of duck breast, Chianti sauce, redcurrants sauteed in beer, and powdered beetroot at the restaurant Radda in Chianti, chefs Mirko Improta and Domenico Russo.

Duck breast with Chianti

Technique: *Roasting in the oven.*

Time: *1 hour 30 minutes.*

Ingredients: *Duck breast (about 900 gr.), red Chianti wine, 2 teaspoons of balsamic vinegar, acacia honey, cinnamon, cloves, rosemary, coarse salt, pepper.*

Place the wine, cloves, balsamic vinegar, cinnamon and honey in a pan and simmer to reduce. Set aside the gravy obtained.

Heat the oven to 200°C.

Clean the duck breast carefully, keeping the skin.

Score it diagonally and massage it with coarse salt and pepper.

Place the breast skin side down in a pan and roast it for ten minutes to lose the fat. Turn the duck breast over and cook for a few more minutes. Remove the fat, turn the breast and cook for another 7/8 minutes.

When cooked, cut the breast into slices and dress it with the Chianti sauce.

The duck

A name common to many migratory birds of the Anatidae family, the duck is a common prey for hunters all over Europe, and Tuscany is no exception, especially in the wetlands that once formed an important part of the region and where these birds find an ideal habitat. The duck has also become a farmyard animal, at least wherever there is a small pond of water nearby. In Tuscany the duck is popularly called *nana*.

Eat it with bread

More than a food, bread is a symbol: a symbol of human work and the fertility of the soil.

Bread is synonymous with civilization. Where there is wheat, there is bread and where there is bread, there is man. We find it in all languages, in all parts of the world, made in a thousand ways, some of them quite unexpected.

Bread is culture, a sign of places and times. We have seen the crops grown on farms in the past: wheat, grape vines, olive trees. Which then meant bread and wine, bread and oil, or even bread and nothing, and that was already a lot in those days. In the changing times, like all cultural bulwarks, even bread is subject to decay. And the decline in this case comes from the long chain of industrial production, perhaps aggravated by relocation of production abroad, with large-scale distribution and its ability to make any product anonymous. This means you might eat bread baked two years ago in a village on the outskirts of Europe and then frozen, transported, defrosted and baked a second time. Bread is not plastic. Uprooted from nature and customs it becomes mediocre and unhealthy. Besides, there's no point in making the world's best prosciutto if we eat it with poor quality bread. Fortunately, some people still hold out and against all logic they get up at three in the morning and bake good bread. Let's see three examples, among the many that enliven the markets in Tuscany.

Bread is synonymous with civilization: where there is wheat there is bread and where there is bread, there is man.

Montegemoli is a castle well off the beaten track between Volterra and the sea, between the hills and the sky. Far from the village, in surreal isolation, the bakery seems to come out of a Nordic fairy tale. A small house on a hill, with smoke coming from the chimney. You might expect to find gnomes there. And instead you find Andrea and Giuseppe who, without uttering a word, knead the dough, lay and light the fire, clean the ovens, bake and turn out the loaves. In short, they bake bread. They make two types, white or wholegrain. The flour changes – it always comes from a trusted mill and is made from stone-ground organic wheat – as does the weight of the loaf, but not the goodness. Proving is slow, the oven is wood-fired, the bread is simple and traditional, fragrant and tasty. A soft crust, bread that remains pleasant even a week after it was first cut. A solid certainty, a small miracle.

Altopascio preserves its vocation as a place of passage. A stopping place on the Via Francigena, between the marshes of the plain and the first buttresses of the Apennines, it retains its shape as a castle. Pilgrims used to pass through it, from door to door, in the shadow of the tower. Today you bypass it rapidly from the highway or a train, because the railway also passes nearby. They could only have invented the Pane del Pellegrino ("Pilgrim's Bread") here. Originally it was a square loaf but today the rules also allow different shapes known as scoletta, coppia, coppione and ruota, meaning anything from a small loaf to a round two-kilo shape. It is made without yeast, without salt, with dough made from Tuscan flour (all kinds of GMO are forbidden) and with the addition of sconcia, a dough that they know how to make only here and which replaces yeast. This is their secret ingredient that makes this bread so special.

Seen in the distance, Montespertoli is a muddle. The houses huddled on the hill, streets that have intersected for a thousand years, nothing that recalls the usual grace of Tuscan towns. Then you enter it and feel at home in that chaos. There is life in that piazza filled with children playing, on that ridge that divides the Valdelsa and offers distant and luminous horizons to the eye. Here, with great passion, a project is being carried out to preserve the ancient cereals and the flour made from them. A broad debate divides opposing factions, but a few, indisputable and solid arguments are enough to present the reasons in its favor. First of all, the ancient cereals are by no means really "ancient". They are strains that go back to before that misunderstood concept of modernity that led agronomists in 1974 to bombard Senatore Cappelli wheat with gamma rays to produce Creso, a wheat better suited to intensive cropping. The cultivation of ancient cereals is subject to a three-year rotation of the land, a practice that is very ancient and avoids the use of pesticides. Furthermore, the organoleptic characteristics of the flour obtained (invariably stone-ground) are significantly better than those of Creso wheat and the production chain involves people strongly motivated and uses greater quantities of land than intensive farming. This might seem a paradox, but it is enough to consider the abandonment of the countryside to understand that a gentler and more widespread agriculture can only be beneficial for the environment. Like good bread for those who know how to appreciate it.

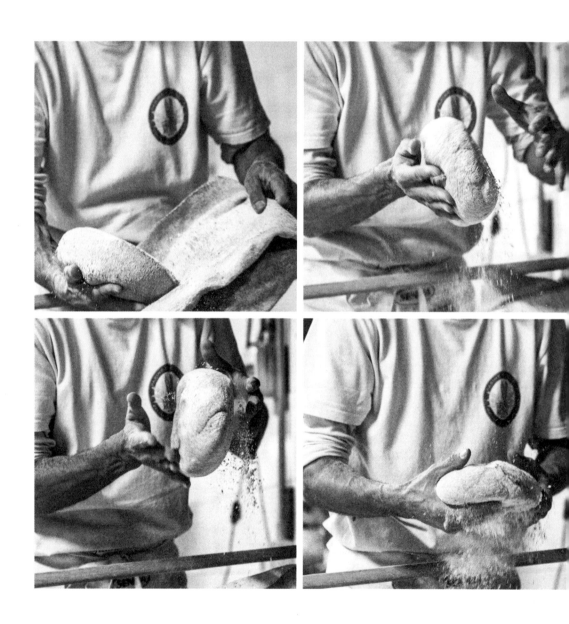

Forno di Montegemoli, Andrea Martini and Giuseppe Zaccheo at work.

Wheat field near the fortified town of Monteriggioni.

. *Heart of veal, Trattoria Il Magazzino, Florence.*

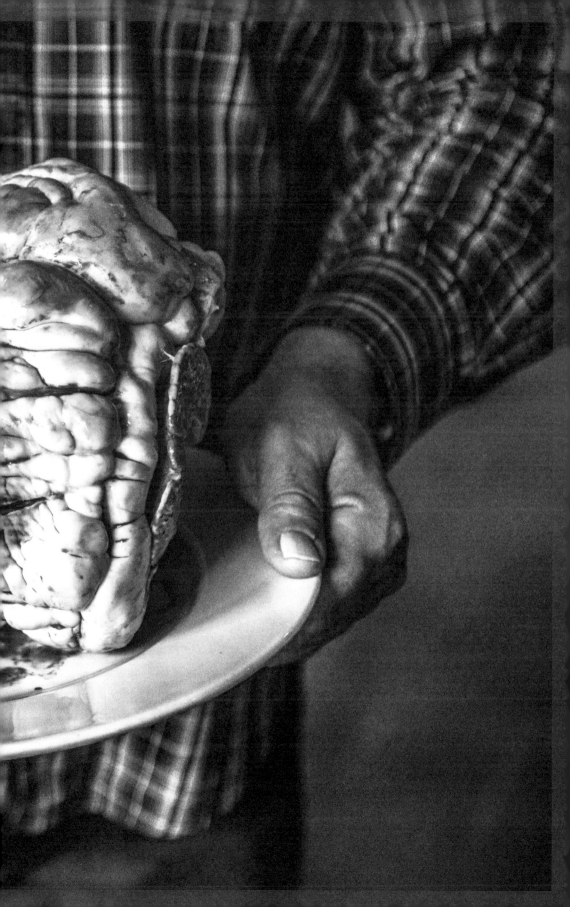

The fifth quarter

Certainly there are poetic cooks, philosopher butchers and gourmet writers. Someone, having to find a term to cover everything that is commonly thrown away, discarded, eliminated from the animals we eat – tripe, testicles, reed tripe, lights, uterus, spleen, tendons, sweetbreads, pluck, rooster's comb and everything else that is neither forequarters nor hindquarters – was inspired to call it the "fifth quarter". As if to say: two plus two equals five. Some aspects of cooking challenge not only vocabulary but math.

In Tuscany the problem arises from the fact that red meat was reserved for the nobles and the wealthy. The poor people had to make do with what was left over at the market after the cooks of the various princes, counts, merchants and bankers had bought up everything else. Which means with little.

Ultimately there remained a whole series of bits and pieces, entrails, organs, glands, giblets that, to be quite frank, are originally a bit disgusting. It's a matter of smell, appearance, function. All stuff that has to be carefully cleaned, washed again and again in running water, cooked with skill and an abundance of herbs that have become the basis of Tuscan cuisine – garlic, celery, onions, carrots, parsley – and which have the task of adding flavor and covering powerful odors, lowering the pH of saturated fats and making even the rooster's combs, the veal tongue and the oxtail digestible.

The *trippaio* is a specialist who cooks and sells all the delicacies that are made from this "fifth quarter". Part wanderer, part fire-eater, he is the healthy embodiment of a hard-to-die Florentine spirit.

Here is an example of offal: abomasum or reed tripe is one of the four stomachs of ruminants and has to be cleaned very carefully before cooking. Once ready it becomes

Sandwich with Lampredotto, prepared by Pier Paolo and Sergio Pollini. Da Nerbone, historic popular restaurant and trippaio at the Central Market, Florence.

Pierpaolo Pollini, son of Sergio, the historic tripe-maker of via dè Macci.

lampredotto, one of the most popular dishes in Florence, which is generally prepared by the *trippaio* and sold in the city streets from a wheeled handcart, being eaten in a *panino* or bread roll.

The trippaio is a specialist who cooks and sells all the delicacies that are made from this "fifth quarter". Part wanderer, part fire-eater, he is the healthy embodiment of a hard-to-die Florentine spirit. You don't go to the trippaio just to eat lampredotto in a bun: you go to see people, listen to the talk, the jokes. You go there to breathe in the aroma of lampredotto which spreads far and wide, fills the senses and impregnates the walls. The aroma of Florence.

Tripe Florentine-style

Technique: *pan cooking.*

Time: *2 hours 30 minutes.*

Ingredients: *7/800 grams of tripe, butter, tomato sauce, half an onion, sage, parsley.*

Chop a segment of onion finely and put it in a pan with the butter and sage and a sprig of parsley.

Brown well and when the onion is colored, add a little tomato paste diluted in water.

Boil for a minute and then add the tripe sliced into thin strips.

Boil slowly for a good two hours, letting the sauce thicken, stirring gently and adding more hot water if necessary.

Serve with grated Parmesan cheese on top.

The dish prepared by Trattoria Il Magazzino, Florence.

Grilled cow's udder in green sauce

Technique: *grilling.*

Time: *15 minutes, plus preparation of the green sauce.*

Ingredients: *800 grams of pre-cooked cow's udder (it can be bought from tripe shops or at the Mercato Centrale).*

For the sauce: parsley, garlic, celery, carrots, onion, anchovy, bread, vinegar, salt, pepper.

Cut the udder into slices about one centimeter thick and cook them on both sides on the grill. Season with the green sauce and serve.

Types of offal and the dishes made from them

by Luca Cai, Trattoria "il Magazzino", Florence

PIECE	CHARACTER	PREPARATION
Brain	Nervous tissue with low caloric content and high fat content. Young calf's brain is used.	Breaded then boiled or fried.
Head	Head of the young calf.	Boiled (in pieces) with herbs in stock or first boiled and then fried.
Cheek	The small muscle that moves the jaw of cattle, it is rich in tissues.	Stewed, boiled or braised, it becomes very tender.
Tongue	Of calf or adult cattle, the weight changes from 1 to 2 kg.	Eaten stewed, with herbs, spices and wine. In winter it is part of a mixed dish of boiled meats while in summer it is pickled.
Diaphragm	The main respiratory muscle of cattle, it is used throughout Italy for making traditional dishes.	In Tuscany it is used in tagliata di manzo, rich in iron.
Heart	Beef heart is eaten and can weigh a few kilos.	The oxheart is toughest, being excellent stewed (in salmì with red wine). Veal's heart is cooked quickly and is excellent fried, grilled and sautéed in a skillet.
Liver	Liver from calves, baby beef or oxen is eaten, as well as from pigs. It is the offal most widely used in cooking.	Cooked in the whole range of ways common in the kitchen.
Kidneys	Kidney of baby beef.	Kidneys are cooked sautéed, reduced with white wine or cognac, eaten deviled or with mustard.
Lights	This is always the lungs of cattle.	Remove the hardest parts and cut into small pieces. Cook them stewed with potatoes or as a soup.
Spleen	Used in all regional and Jewish cuisines, it is usually peeled and thinly sliced or ground.	In Tuscany it is also cooked fresh on the grill.
Udder	Cow's udder.	Boiled for 5 hours, excellent with croutons with green sauce and mayonnaise, or grilled, but also fried and sautéed in a pan Livorno-style.
Testicles	Bull's testicles.	Skinned and blanched for five minutes in boiling water, then cut across into discs, they are served breaded and fried.

PIECE	CHARACTER	PREPARATION
Innards	These are the purged and cleaned intestines.	Grilled or fried.
Tripe	In cattle, the stomach is made up of four distinct cavities: RUMEN (*Ciapa, Croce, Larga, Panzone*) is the thickest and broadest part of the tripe, making up about 80 percent of the whole bovine stomach. RETICULUM (*Beretta, Cuffia, Nido d'Ape*) has a spongy, cap-shaped appearance. OMASUM (*Centopezzi, Foiolo, Libretto, Millefogli, Centopelli*) is the widest and leanest part of the tripe and has a typical lamellar structure with innumerable folds suggesting an open book. ABOMASUM (*Caglio, Francese, Frezza, Lampredotto, Quaglietto, Ricciola*) is the only cavity equivalent to the actual stomach, the one closest to the intestine.	Cooked in endless ways in all traditional cuisine. The most famous dish is *Lampredotto*, a popular street food in Florence.
Uterus	The womb of the cow.	Boiled and seared on the hotplate, marinated hot with garlic, parsley, salt and abundant pepper. *Alla Francesina*, it is cooked with onion.
Feet	Muscles of the lower part of the legs of a calf.	Rich in collagen, when boiled they make gelatinous stocks. Boneless, they can be used in salads and stewed dishes.
Tail	Of ox or calf, it is made up of muscles and bones rich in cartilage.	It enriches stews and braised meats with very succulent sauces and makes a fine sauce for pasta.
Bones and Marrow	Even if they do not really belong to offal, bones and marrow have played an important role in the kitchen since ancient times. They are used in stocks and broths because they increase flavor and mineral content. In addition, marrow fats are monounsaturated and can reduce LDL cholesterol levels.	In traditional cuisine the bone marrow, not to be confused with the spinal cord, is appreciated in many dishes such as soup, mixed boiled meats, osso buco, or stuffed with meat where it acts as a binder and seasoning.

Trippai in Florence

1 - **I' Bandito** - Piazza Pier Vittori

2 - **Il Trippaio di Porta Romana** - Piazzale di Porta Romana

3 - **I' Trippaio di Firenze** - Via Ugo Forscolo

4 - **Trippaio del Porcellino** - Mercato del Porcellino

5 - **I' Trippaio fiorentino** - Via Gioberti

6 - **Antico trippaio** - Piazza Cimatori

7 - **Nerbone** - Mercato Centrale

8 - **Pier Paolo e Sergio Pollini** - Via De' Macci

9 - **I' Trippaio di San Frediano** - Piazzale De' Neri

10 - **I' Trippaio di Sant'Ambrogio** - Mercato di Sant'Ambrogio

11 - **Lupen & Margo** - Via Dell'Ariento

12 - **La Tripperia delle Cure** - Piazza delle Cure

13 - **Eredi Lorenzo Nigro** - Mercato Centrale

14 - **Il Lampredottore** - Via Caccini

15 - **Aurelio** - Piazza Tanucci

16 - **Trippaio di Montini** - Viale De Amicis

17 - **Chiosco del Galluzzo** - Piazza del Galluzzo

18 - **Mario di Piazza Alberti** - Piazza Alberti

19 - **Da' Vinattieri** - Via Santa Margherita

Veal heart scallops au naturel

Technique: *pan cooking.*

Time: *10 minutes.*

Ingredients: *600 grams of veal heart, vegetable or meat stock, salt, pepper.*

Cut the heart into slices as thin as possible, fry in olive oil on both sides and deglaze with stock to make the sauce thicker or thinner to taste. Add salt and pepper and serve.

Bull's testicles fried in sauce

Technique: *frying and cooking in a pan.*

Time: *20 minutes.*

Ingredients: *Bull's testicles (available from tripe stores or at the central market or in Sant'Ambrogio), garlic, parsley, chili, tomato paste, egg, breadcrumbs, red wine, olive oil, salt, pepper.*

Cut the testicles into slices, dip them in egg and breadcrumbs, fry them in olive oil. Add wine when they turn golden.

In a pan prepare a sauce of garlic, parsley, chilis and tomato paste and cook the fried slices of testicles in it until it has absorbed the sauce.

Stefano Bencistà Falorni engaged in dividing the hog, the first task in butchering it.

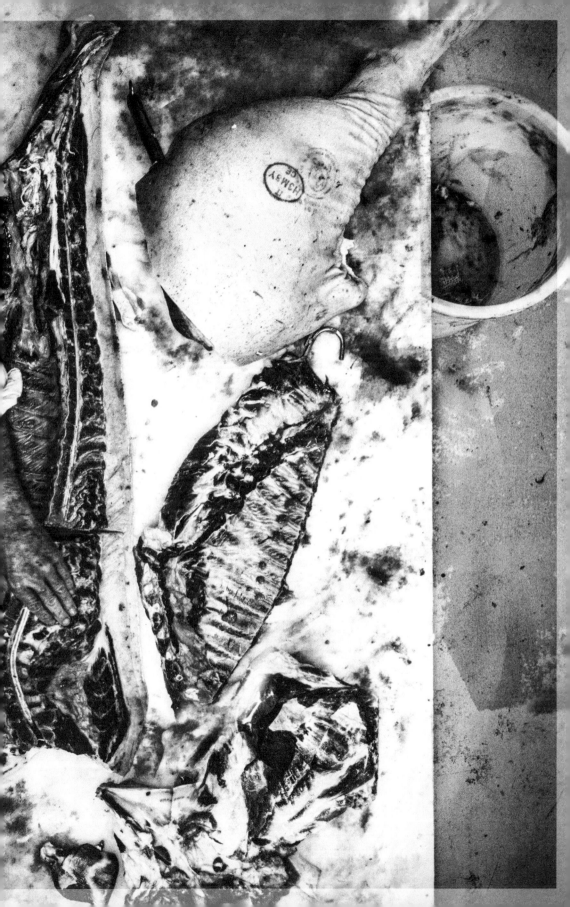

Sheep, lambs, rams

Now we're going to talk about islands. But forget Elba, Giglio or Giannutri. Sheep, in the Tuscan gastronomic panorama, means above all cheese. But this is a book about meat and so in the case of sheep – if sheep means lamb or mutton – we have to talk about islands. Culinary islands.

The mysterious island is Zeri. Zeri is a town in Lunigiana, in the northwest of the region. This is an out-of-the-way place and it takes an effort to get there. Zeri does not have a real center. It is a cluster of hamlets scattered across a mountain ridge wedged between Tuscany, Liguria and Emilia Romagna. Here the roads and countryside are of two types: uphill or downhill. Perhaps this is why so many sheep are still raised in these parts. In certain periods, even quite recent times, there were three thousand sheep for every thousand inhabitants. This may not sound many compared to the 480,000 head of sheep in Tuscany. But they certainly make an impression, because they are rare, valuable, indigenous sheep of a recognized breed and Slow Food has declared the region a "presidium". Their peculiarity is in their milk, rich in proteins, due to the hardy nature of these sheep and the landforms of the region where they live: impervious, but also wild and natural, so that the Zerasca breed of sheep are out at pasture almost all the year round. And they produce fantastic milk. But the locals do not make cheese out of that high-protein milk – they joke that if they did it would all roll down into the valleys. They simply rear the lambs on it, their true purpose in raising these sheep. Zerasco lambs have tender, fragrant, exquisite flesh. It is true that it takes a heart of stone to kill them, but the tradition comes from the distant past and the distant past was hunger and fatigue so intense that it remains legible in the landscape. And a certain inclination towards harshness and pragmatism is part of this landscape, including the people.

Yet lamb in Tuscany was a common and popular meat. Today people eat lamb chops and little else.

And then there is the testo. A testo is a cast iron pot with a cast iron lid. It weighs as much as a washing machine and is very popular around here for cooking anything. It seems that they carried it around like a camp kitchen, in the times of transhumance and migration. A little fire was enough and they could even cook stones in it, so to speak. They are made

A flock of sheep shelters from the sun under a cork oak in Maremma.

Flock of sheep near Buonconvento.

at Pontremoli and used only in this valley. You will never find anything of the sort outside Lunigiana. And Zeri lamb is cooked in it. Slow cooking over low heat with herbs and flavorings. Well worth the trip.

Yet lamb in Tuscany was a common and popular meat. Today people eat lamb chops and little else. But Giovanni Villani in his Chronicle listed all the foodstuffs necessary to supply the city of Florence in the years between the thirteenth and fourteenth centuries: "The city needed, of oxen and calves some four thousand; sixty thousand geldings and sheep; she-goats and bucks, twenty thousand; pigs, thirty thousand..."

Adding together geldings, sheep, goats and bucks, it can be easily deduced that the flesh of sheep was widely consumed in the city, much more than beef or pork. Too bad Villani doesn't tell us anything about poultry.

Another less exotic, more urban island is Campi Bisenzio and its countryside. For example: "Sant'Angelo a Lecore, the town of sheep" already fills the air with light-hearted charm. And the natives are likeable, rather rough. They never got lost even when Campi was incorporated into a network of roads, warehouses, junctions, shopping centers... They stayed there with just a few certainties, including cooking lamb and mutton. Many recipes, even strange ones (in these parts, before reclaiming the swamps to build interchanges and sheds, the people used to eat frogs) among which stewed mutton was notable, complete with a popular competition to decide each year who made it best. But the essence of their spirit was fully captured by that genius who invented – and it could only have happened here, between via Pistoiese and the west – the mutton burger.

Lamb fricassee

Technique: *pan cooking.*

Time: *1 hour 15 minutes.*

Ingredients: *1.2 kg lamb, 2 cloves garlic, rosemary, 1 tablespoon flour, 1 glass of white wine, 4 egg yolks, 1 lemon, olive oil, salt, pepper, stock.*

Put half a glass of olive oil in a pan with the whole garlic cloves and a sprig of rosemary and fry.

Making sure the garlic doesn't burn, add the lamb in small pieces, sprinkle them with flour and brown over high heat.

Add the wine and reduce it, add salt and pepper and continue cooking, adding stock from time to time.

While waiting for it to cook, in a small bowl, beat the egg yolks with the lemon juice.

When the lamb is cooked (about one hour) pour over it the sauce, stir well and remove from the heat.

Serve covered with the sauce.

Preparation of the traditional roast in the testi during the Zerasca sheep festival, Zeri, Lunigiana.

Shoulder of lamb with artichokes

Technique: *pan cooking.*

Time: *1 hour 30 minutes.*

Ingredients: *1.2 kg of shoulder of lamb,
3/5 artichokes, garlic, olive oil, rosemary, white wine,
tomato sauce, stock, salt, pepper.*

---

*In a pan put olive oil and 4/5 cloves of peeled garlic
with some sprigs of rosemary and brown them.
Be careful that the garlic does not burn and add
the meat.*

*Cook it until it turns a nice brown color,
sprinkle with wine and reduce.*

*Clean the artichokes, removing the tough leaves,
cut them into wedges and add them to the meat.*

*Cook for 5 minutes and add the tomato, salt and
pepper and cook for about 1 hour, gradually adding
the stock.*

Roast lamb

Technique: *oven roasting.*

Time: *1 hour 20 minutes.*

Ingredients: *1.5 kg leg and loin, rosemary,
garlic, salt, pepper.*

*Score the meat in several places and add salt, pepper,
rosemary and minced garlic.*

*Salt all the meat, put olive oil in a pan and roast at
180°C for an hour, turning it 3/4 times.*

Once cooked, cut into pieces and serve.

At dinner with Dante

Asked what was the best food in the world, Dante replied: the egg! The anecdote has it that the questioner went off in disdain, only to come back out of the blue a year later and complete the question: With what? With salt. Nothing else. It's hardly surprising that Dante put the gluttons in hell to rot under eternal freezing and stinking rain. Or if his Divine Comedy mentions more than fifty animals – in the form of direct narrative or metaphor – and almost none of these can be eaten. Maybe as hunters: hawk, sparrowhawk, creatures that eat rather than being eaten.

You choose for yourselves, but if I had lived in Tuscany in the early fourteenth century, I would have got someone else to invite me to dinner. For example, an evening at the home of Folgore da San Gimignano, who never missed an opportunity to declaim the praises of a joyful and spendthrift life, though not so scandalous as that of his countryman Cecco Angiolieri. All the same, he knew how to have fun:

> And every Wednesday, as the swift days move,
> Pheasant and peacock-shooting out of doors
> You'll have, and multitude of hares to course,
> And after you come home, good cheer enough;
>
> And sweetest ladies at the board above,
> Children of kings and counts and senators;
> And comely-favor'd youthful bachelors
> To serve them, bearing garlands, for true love.
>
> And still let cups of gold and silver ware,
> Runlets of vernage-wine and wine of Greece,
> Comfits and cakes be found at bidding there;
>
> And let your gifts of birds and game increase;
> And let all those who in your banquet share
> Sit with bright faces perfectly at ease.

In those years, somewhere, the first cooking manuals were also being written, and "eating well" was acquiring an identity of its own. Other poets – Boccaccio among them – treated

Miracle of the Golden Pitcher, Barga cathedral, bas-relief above the side door. Sculpture attributed to Biduino 12th century.

Duccio di Buoninsegna, The Last Supper painted on a panel on the back of the Maestà in Siena cathedral.

the theme with more appropriate lightness. Just to give an example: Ciacco, the glutton whom we have already met doleful and complaining in the Divine Comedy (Canto VI), returns as the protagonist in one of the days of the Decameron, where he is the victim of a practical joke connected with his proverbial gluttony and then devises a refined revenge for that joke:

Biondello cheateth Ciacco of a dinner, whereof the other craftily avengeth himself, procuring him to be shamefully beaten. (Decameron, Day IX novel 8)

And Boccaccio again attracts Calandrino to the land of Bengodi with these enticements from Maso del Saggio and Buffalmacco:

"Here the vines are tied up with sausages and a goose is to be had for a farthing and a gosling into the bargain, and that there was a mountain all of grated Parmesan cheese, whereon abode folk who did nothing but make macaroni and ravioli and cook them in capon-broth, after which they threw them down thence and whoso got most thereof had most; and that hard by ran a rivulet of vernage, the best that ever was drunk, without a drop of water therein."

It is an apotheosis of flavor and abundance, which glories in excess. A far cry from egg with a little salt. Here we have absolute indulgence, a shame and a scandal. Another Florentine, a contemporary and friend of Boccaccio, sets things to rights. This was Francesco Petrarch who fell madly in love with Laura, but was still lucid enough to write a precise analysis of the "dinner of the busy man and that of the lonely man", a eulogy of frugality but without renouncing taste, abhorring sophistication and extolling authenticity in a way that sounds like a manifesto of today's Italian cuisine. In the midst of this description of the different dinners and settings and moods and feelings – now noisy and heavy, now light and quiet – Petrarch presents a small maxim that today you might find on a chocolate wrapper, but none the less acceptable for that:

"That the greatest and true wealth consists in not desiring anything, the greatest power in not being afraid of anything."

Panorama from Lucardo.

Berti cutlery, Scarperia.

Cutting irons

Between Florence and Bologna there is an ancient, compact and beautiful town. It's called Scarperia. The name prompts the visitor to think, surely shoes (*scarpe* in Italian) must be made here. No, not shoes. This place, at the start of its history, was called "Castello a La Scarperia", meaning on the scarp or cliff. Around the "castle on the cliff" built in the early 14th century at the behest of the Florentine government, a village grew up. In front of the castle ran a road that went north (or south, depending on where you were heading). At any rate, the comings and goings of trade, stopovers for caravans and pilgrims, workers, troops. At a certain point people started talking about the knives of Scarperia. The earliest document, a will dating from 1479, confirms that excellent knives had been made here for a long time. Scarperia is the land of knives.

Having clarified the name, the question remains. Why are knives made in Scarperia? Answer: Nobody knows. They just make them, they always have made them, and they also make them well. That seems to about sum it up.

In the fifties in Scarperia there were 44 cutlers' shops and 10 scissors makers.

Come to think of it, however, there was no iron here. It had to be brought in. And the wood for the handles? It wasn't special here, like ox horn, which was found everywhere. So? Why here? Berti, from a family of cutlers for five generations, suggests the answer lies in taxation. The Signoria declared that anyone from Florence who moved to live in the new outpost would be exempt from taxes for ten years. It seems that many Florentine cutlers moved to Mugello. Then Berti wanders off the subject and says that steel today is too technical and the hardening has to be precise. It's no longer like in his grandfather's time, when they hardened the steel in the dark by telling the temperature of the blade by the color of the incandescent metal.

You persist in trying to discover the real reason, but he tells you about ox horn and explains that the tip is the best part for making a knife handle, even if it is complicated to work and a pair of horns only gives you two handles, while you can get ten from the lower part of the horn.

You bring him back to history and at that point he tells you the stories told by those who were old when he was a child. It appears in the fifties at Scarperia there were still 44 cutlers' shops and 10 scissors makers. It was a world that still reflected the ancient ways, and in being ancient it had its beauty, but also its limit. It was a community that grew up along a road and the surnames and origins of many inhabitants were unknown. They were only called by their nicknames – Dondolo, Olivo, Masino, Pipino, il Mangia... a nickname, a story. Then many others with a name and surname, but short of money. There was little money and to do the work it was customary for them to lend each other some of their tools.

In short, Scarperia was not filled with the clashing of anvils and hammers busily forging blades for princes and knights. They mainly made working knives. Cheap knives for the poor, shipped to the South. Sicily and Calabria were the main markets.
Everything came to an end soon after. In the 1960s almost all the workshops closed down, the scissors disappeared, the few who had a larger resources than others survived.

It took intelligence, tenacity and a little luck to build the myth. They started from the production of a regional knife, the "Maremmano", which paved the way for this successful series here in Scarperia, the soul and history of the knife and in some way the city has also been rebuilt. The stones were already there, it was only a question of restoring their role and character.

What followed – the reopening of many shops, design, success, exports, rivalries, foreigners – come to think of it, would be commonplace in a world that has become so small. But this is a special case: orphans of their past, in Scarperia they found themselves reinventing the present present and they did it well. The hope is that that the future will once again be out of the box: a little skewed but true, shiny and... sharp.

Group of Chianina cattle at the entrance to a byre, Fattoria di Trequanda.

Chianina and Maremmana

In Tuscany there are two cattle breeds that matter: the Chianina and the Maremmana.

Like two prima donnas, they go out of their way to be noticed. One for its gigantic size, the other for its monumental horns. Both with a very elegant bearing, as befits queens.

Historically they inhabit two very different territories, regions from which they take their name and with which, in some way, they have entered into symbiosis.

Imposing and placid, the Chianina embodies the spirit of the plain that it inhabits, the Val di Chiana. Broad spaces, fertile land, well suited to slowness and agriculture. A tireless, docile breed, capable of working and renowned all over the world for the purity of its white coat and the goodness of its meat. It is often identified as the only breed of cattle from which the famous "Fiorentina" steaks can be made. This is not exactly true, but if there is an Olympus of cattle, the Chianina has already conquered a place of honor for centuries.

Rustic and reserved, the Maremmana blends with the scrub that separates the sea from the hilly buttresses of the Maremma. The rest is land reclaimed from the marshes with the back-breaking effort of men and animals. It is through the history of this conquest that the Maremmana has been appreciated for its strength and endurance. Today, to use a term in vogue, we might call it "resilient", and in fact the Maremmana adapts to everything. It fails to tolerate only one thing: living in captivity. The Maremmana cattle graze freely tended by the legendary *butteri* (herdsmen) on horseback.

The butteri are the legendary herders of Maremmana cattle.

Ossi buchi of veal with white rice

Technique: *cooking in a pan.*

Time: *1 hour 20 minutes.*

Ingredients: *ossi buchi (veal shanks cut across the shin), olive oil, butter, water, two sweet onions (the cipolle di Certaldo are best), marsala, tomato sauce, carrots, stock, rice, salt.*

In a fairly large pan put plenty of olive oil, two big knobs of butter, a little water and the finely chopped onions and brown them.

Flour the ossi buchi and arrange them in the pan, browning them well on both sides, add a glass of Marsala wine and reduce it, then add a good quantity of tomato sauce and 4/5 carrots cut into small cubes.

Season with salt and pepper, cook in a covered pan for over an hour, adding stock from time to time.

Meanwhile boil the rice in salted water, drain it and season it with butter.

The rice should be served beside the ossi buchi seasoned with the cooking sauce.

Trequanda Chianina stud farm with the bull Gelsomino da Badia. Traditionally a bull bred on its home farm is only given a first name, while if it comes from a different farm it is also given a surname, as in this case.

Ancient ornaments on the irons for tethering horses,
Palazzo Borgia, Pienza.

Veal sauce

Technique: *pan cooking.*

Time: *3 hours 15 minutes.*

Ingredients: *400 g minced veal, olive oil, salt, pepper, two celery ribs, 1 carrot, 1 small onion, basil, a sprig of parsley, red wine, tomato sauce.*

In a pan with half a glass of olive oil put the chopped vegetables and cook until they are soft, add the meat and brown well turning often.

Season with salt, pepper, pour in the wine and deglaze. Add the tomato and when it starts to boil, lower the heat.

Cover the pan and simmer for three hours. Use the sauce for dressing pasta.

Roast beef

Technique: pan cooking.

Time: 1 hour.

Ingredients: 1 kg lean beef (sirloin), sage, garlic, rosemary, salt, pepper, olive oil.

Chop together sage, rosemary and garlic.

Put the olive oil in a deep pan.

Make small incisions on the meat and add the seasoning.

Put the pan over high heat and brown on all sides for 10/15 minutes. The meat should crackle while cooking. Cover and lower the heat, cook for another 15/20 minutes.

Let the meat rest in the pan for 15 minutes, cut and serve with the gravy on top.

San Rossore estate, cows at pasture with calves.

Tuscan chuck steak casserole

Technique: *pan cooking.*

Time: *2 hours 20 minutes.*

Ingredients: *800 gr of chuck steak, pepper, sage, rosemary, garlic, olive oil, 4/500 grams of tomato sauce, onion, carrot, celery.*

Chop together sage, garlic, rosemary and sprig the meat in two or three places.

Mix the salt, pepper and olive oil and all the chopped herbs in a pan. Brown them and when they are golden add the meat and brown it on all sides.

Add a glass of red wine and let it evaporate, add the tomato, lightly salt, pepper and cook with the lid on for at least 2 hours, turning the meat often.

Slice the meat. Pass the gravy through a sieve and use it to dress the meat.

Mario Mariani, experienced terracotta craftsman, Impruneta.

Firing bricks in a small kiln.

Beef with black pepper

Technique: *oven braising.*

———————————

Time: *preparation 10 minutes; minimum cooking 3-4 hours.*

———————————

Ingredients: *1 kg of Chianina flank, 1 lt. Chianti, black pepper, 5 cloves of unpeeled garlic, sliced Tuscan bread, sage, rosemary, salt.*

———————————

Cut the meat into bite-sized pieces in a crock pot.

Add the unpeeled garlic cloves, salt, pepper, sage and rosemary.

Cover with red wine and cook over moderate heat in the oven or on the hob, until the meat is really soft.

Peposo all'Imprunetina prepared by Trattoria Burde, Florence.

NON SERVIAMO
FIORENTINE
BEN COTTE
RISPETTIAMO LE
NOSTRE TRADIZIONI
VIVA LA CICCIA
BONA

Ristorante La Selva di Frena, Firenzuola.

Old butcher's shop sign at Montisi.

Veal cheeks braised in Chianti

Technique: *roasting in pan and skillet.*

Time: *3 hours.*

Ingredients: *4 veal cheeks, pepper, salt, olive oil, beef stock, bay leaf, rosemary, sage, mushrooms, two ribs of celery, dried porcini (cep mushrooms), 2 onions, 300 grams of carrots, two glasses of red wine.*

Soak the mushrooms in warm water.

Clean the veal cheeks by removing excess fat.

Season with salt and pepper and brown in a very hot pan with a drizzle of olive oil on both sides.

Dice the celery, carrots and onion and put them in a pan with 2/3 tablespoons of olive oil, brown them for a few minutes, add the veal cheeks and cook for a few minutes.

Add the wine, deglaze and add the mushrooms with their filtered water and stock to cover.

Add sage, rosemary and bay leaf.

Cover and cook over low heat for 2 hours 30 minutes, adding stock if it gets too dry.

Use the sauce to season the meat when serving.

Braised cheek prepared by the chef Daniele Falciani, Ristoro L' Antica Scuderia, Badia a Passignano.

Lesso Rifatto or Francesina, Trattoria Il Magazzino, Florence.

Boiled beef with onions

Technique: pan cooking.

Time: 1 hour.

Ingredients: 500 g of ready boiled beef, 3 onions, tomato, celery, carrot, olive oil, salt, pepper.

Put abundant olive oil and the three finely chopped onions in a pan, let them soften gently together with the well chopped celery and carrot.

When everything has taken on a nice amber color, add the meat cut into coarse slices.

Add salt and pepper and season well. Now add a glass of tomato sauce to cover and cook for another 15 minutes.

Breaded veal steak

Technique: *frying in a pan.*

———————————

Time: *45 minutes.*

———————————

Ingredients: *veal steaks on the bone (rib steak), 3 eggs, breadcrumbs.*

———————————

Slightly detach the bone (say for half its length) and with a meat mallet flatten it out until it is twice the size.

Heat the olive oil in the pan.

Beat the 3 eggs with a little salt, add the meat and stir well so that the egg adheres completely.

Roll the steaks twice in the breadcrumbs.

When the olive oil is very hot, add the slices of meat and turn several times. When they have turned a hazelnut color they are ready.

Dry on kitchen paper, salt and serve.

Breaded veal steak prepared by the Chef Vincenzo Dilorenzo, Ristorante Regina Bistecca, Florence.

Steak tartare

Technique: *seasoned cold.*

Time: *20 minutes.*

Ingredients: *500/600 grams of meat (fillet, sirloin), salt, pepper, olive oil, egg, and Dijon mustard to taste.*

Cut the meat into slices, then into strips, then into small squares (better still, get the butcher to cut it for you).

Place it in a container, add salt and pepper and 3 spoonfuls of olive oil. Mix well and shape the tartar using the special ring or with a shallow, wide-mouthed glass.

To each of these 4 forms add the egg yolk without the white.

Dijon mustard, if desired, is placed next to the tartar and not on top. Never.

Fire

Bronze melts at 900°C, gold at 1065°C, steak cooks at 500°C. More or less.

Many think that the word "barbecue" is English. No, barbecue is a transliteration of the Spanish term Barbacoa which in turn derives from a word indigenous to the island of Haiti, where Spanish navigators discovered this cooking technique was common and apparently, also involved forms of cannibalism. Perhaps this impressed them deeply and since then everything cooked on a live fire has become a barbecue.

But here in Tuscany they call it a grigliata or say alla griglia. If you are lucky enough to see a master of the grill at work, you will realize it is more than just a matter of fire and iron.

At first it might seem a rather casual matter. A little wood, a match and away. But then there are all sorts of things to watch out for.

To prepare the right fire, the first thing to do is ask in the kitchen what time they mean to eat and how many people will be coming.

Start from what no one can see: draughts. You have to avoid draughts. If air passes below, it will fan a flame and a flame is no good for cooking. Then from what you see: the hob, which has to be smooth, solid, above all it should not let the air pass underneath. A brick hob is best. An iron barbecue is no good. It always has a drawer for the ash and the air passes through it. No iron. Iron is fine for the grill, which has to be heavy because it laid over the fire and iron melts at 1538°C, but already at 700°C it can be forged. At 500°C it is weakened and at 500°C it cooks steak. A grill that is too light after a while becomes badly warped and imprecise. Without precision there is no perfection.

But more than iron or brick, the important thing is the firewood. No poplar or spruce because they give off a low heat. It can't be cypress, which explodes. It can't be olive or wood from a tree grown too close to a river: fast growing, with broad fibers, it goes up like straw. So what wood is best? It has to be oak. Hard wood from a tree far from a river, cut down a year before. This is definite. It should not be too fresh or too dry. Or else use coal.

The oven of "Pane di Montegemoli".

Old woodsman in traditional workwear.

Not charcoal – horror! – coal. Good coal. And to light it never use alcohol, least of all – sacrilege! – those smelly white firelighters used by city dwellers.

Then there is the whole question of how this wood should be burned: stacked, horizontal, vertical, laid crisscross… It sounds like nonsense, but the subject is serious.

Falorni says that the first thing to do is to ask in the kitchen what time to eat and how many people will be coming. It is essential to size up the fire and make the time coincide with the cooking time. Then, at the right moment, light it.

Falorni argues that the best method is to gather the wood into a bundle of logs, place them vertically and burn them from below. Combustion will be uniform, with a compact and homogeneous block of embers. A minute before putting the meat on to cook, you should undo the bundle and spread the embers neatly across the hob, then place the grill on top.

Place the grill low above the embers to cook steak, a little higher for other kinds of meat. With a veil of ash on the embers if you want to cook skewers of meat and not burn them. It calls for a lifetime of experience in lighting of the fire, touching the meat to feel if it is cooked (never pierce it with a fork!). Judging with a clinical eye the shades of red and ash to estimate the temperature, gauge the distances, calculate the time. It is a series of gestures that go beyond memory, following, goodness knows how, the inner instruction booklet that we have handed down to us from prehistoric times, from the discovery of the first fire, from the evolutionary leap.

And then you understand that the search for perfection is not in vain and even has something mystical about it. It is a dutiful, solemn homage to food, to fire, to what we have been from the dawn of humanity to the present and will continue to be, as long as there is a house with a fireplace, a fire burning, a man bending over the grill…

If you want to identify someone who is good for nothing, get him to light a fire.

La fiorentina

It's not that in Florence they take a cow, cut off the steaks and throw the rest away. The rest is cut up and cooked just they same as everyone else does, the usual things. Here we are talking about exceptions and not rules. But steak is an exception and deserves space.

I'll say it again: "la Fiorentina" is a football team. Or a lady who lives in Florence. *Bistecca* is steak, A T-bone, four fingers thick.

But then you cross over to the other side of the Apennines and *bistecca* – the same cut of meat – is called a *braciola*. And here things get complicated. For us a braciola is what others call a fettina. In short, it can be difficult for Italians to understand each other.

The custom of calling our steak fiorentina emerged from the shadow of a planetary tragedy that occurred in the mid-1980s, later known as "Mad Cow disease". To be precise, it wasn't the cow that was mad, it was the people who from greed, superficiality and recklessness forced – through the complex alchemy of fodder – British cows into cannibalism. From there the disease spread, especially through the media because our cattle, historical Italian breeds and cattle reared in Italy have always been healthy, as was later recognized in 2008 by the Standing Committee for the Food Chain of the European Union, later replaced by the EFSA (European Food Safety Authority).

Don't cook sausages, poultry on the same grill. Steak is a prima donna. It wants a hob all to itself.

In any case, they were difficult years in these parts. From 2001 to 2006 the sale of meat adjacent to the vertebrae of cattle was prohibited. And a boneless steak is no longer a steak. To explain the exception and defend the tradition, it was decided, to make it clear, call the steak a *fiorentina* or, with an acceptable compromise, *bistecca alla fiorentina*. The problem solved, the name remained. And so it was.

Bistecca alla Fiorentina prepared by Paolo Bacciotti, Ristorane Tullio a Montebeni.

Bistecca alla Fiorentina being cooked.

The *bistecca alla fiorentina* is one of the 17-19 parts in which you can cut the loin of baby beef (if male) or a heifer (if female): 5/6 steaks in the fillet, 12/14 in the rib – without the fillet – but with tastier meat. And here the debate could be endless, influenced by personal tastes, experiences, eras. For example Pellegrino Artusi argued that real *bistecca* could only be fillet steak from Chianina cattle. But he wrote that in 1870, and given the time and the boundaries of that world, he was probably right. No longer today, when we live a wider horizon, and the influences and fusions are stronger.

From different kinds of cattle can come steak with different qualities of flavor and softness. The important thing is that the breed is of quality and the loin is cut skillfully. Never wedge-shaped, so as not to compromise regular cooking, in pieces of sufficient thickness because "less than four fingers it's not steak, it's a carpaccio."

How to cook, letter to Pellegrino Artusi from an anonymous Tuscan "bisteccaio".

Dear and Illustrious Artusi,
I read with great pleasure and interest your prized Science in the Kitchen and the Art of Eating Well, still so relevant even though 130 years – more or less – have gone by since it was first published. From those pages we still have a lot to learn, even those of us who have been in the profession for a long time. I only allow myself, having read with disappointment that in your recipe 556, dedicated to bistecca alla fiorentina, you recommend putting a knob of butter on the steak after cooking, to remind you and the readers of the golden rules for cooking the bistecca alla fiorentina to perfection. You who have crossed the Apennines should realize that ridge is a border between two worlds: the world of butter and the world of oil, understood as olive oil of course, and when the steak is already cut, we put olive oil on it. And sometimes we do it alla frantoiana, really splurging the olive oil, and it's marvelous, a far cry from rancid butter!

First of all the fire. I've have already said this, but perhaps it would be as well to repeat it. It must be made of the embers of a hard wood like oak, or good coal and must be at least six/seven centimeters high. The grill must be large and sturdy and heated a few minutes before you start cooking. Between the embers and the grill there should be two to three centimeters, no more. Steak wants live heat. When you place the steak on the grill (with tongs, never with a fork) it should sizzle and stick to the iron. After a few minutes, touching it gently with the tongs, the steak will come off the grill without any resistance except for its weight. That means it's done on that side. Then turn it over like turning the page of a book, so that it rests on a different part of the grill, beneath which there are plenty of live embers. While the steak is cooking on the other side, sprinkle plenty of salt (not too fine, not too coarse) – and pepper for those who want it – on the part already cooked. Wait until the second side it done to turn the steak over and salt it again, and then tap it to remove the excess salt.

Fillet steak calls for extra care, since it cooks differently from the rib and you will have to remodel the embers to optimize the cooking. Then you should be careful not to cook sausage or poultry on the same grill. Steak is a prima donna and wants a fire all to itself.

Once cooked, the problem of cutting arises, which you, dear Pellegrino, have probably omitted due to distraction or forgetfulness, but the delicacy of the theme requires me to try to make good this omission, because unless you cut it properly you cannot care for meat. The blade must be smooth, not a serrated blade, otherwise the meat becomes frayed and loses substance and with it protein. The best knife is one with a slightly curved edge, rather like a scimitar, so you use the whole blade, from the handle to the tip, and with a softer movement. If the knife is really sharp, the meat does not even notice the cut and remains compact and whole on the tip of the fork.

Regina Bistecca, the charcoal grill, chef Vincenzo Dilorenzo.

Bistecca alla fiorentina prepared by Paolo Bacciotti, Ristorante Tullio at Montebeni.

Red, the right wine

The feet have instinct, the hands have memory, the body knows things we don't know.

Nobody should take it ill, but it has to be said that as long as wine was a peasant matter, nobody made a big thing of it. Of course it was always on the table and people drank it, but it was food rather than drink, and little was said about it. Good, not so good: there probably wasn't much more to say. Even deciding what to plant in the vineyard went by rule of thumb and depended on a thousand stories, certainly not on the awareness of where you wanted to go.

Then the concept of "quality" came from the industrial world. In 1980s some things had to be put in order. In agriculture, the oenologists arrived and people began to work in the vineyard and the winery with an eye to quality. They realized that a wine could be something more and better than "wholesome". It could convey aromas and perfumes, enhance food and represent the personality of the land like few other things. Wonderful.

Since then, on the wave of the wonder, there has been a proliferation of labels and speeches, a whirling of glasses, a flourishing of experts. Very nice and great fun, richness and wonder. But at some point we have to ask a question. Why is it better to drink red wine with red meat. Why?

I've asked a lot of people about this and the answer was always vague: aroma, the bouquet, aroma, the aftertaste. Or habit. As an answer it seemed lacking, and they even handed it down as gospel. So I decide to go and beard the wolf in his lair, asking the question of one of those who have intuited, interpreted and conducted all this wonder. I find him at Greve in Chianti, in his office a stone's throw from the square. You immediately understand that it is not a lawyer's office. It has a white counter with glasses aligned, a stone sink and ceramic tiles with vine branches. He is called Stefano Chioccioli and I put my question to him. The lapidary answer: polyphenols. In red wine there are polyphenols, in white there aren't.

And then, quietly, with precise words he explains that polyphenols are molecules of organic origin – among much else they are also good for the health – contained in fruit, vegetables, wood and the peel of black grapes. And since red wine is made by soaking the skins, while in making white the skins are discarded, this explains the reason for the presence of polyphenols in red wine. He explains that they have an elective link with proteins: red meat, in fact. And they enhance its flavor and make it more digestible.

Nature is strength, energy: it transforms things following a tumultuous and unstoppable process of change.

Then you realize that aromas and perfumes have very little to do with it. The body has already chosen for us through all that paraphernalia of unconscious knowledge known as the ancestral, unconscious memory, which then, through experience, becomes culture.

The question of the grape variety is even more complex. Speaking of red wines in Tuscany there are dozens of them, including 13 DOC and 13 DOCG wines. An impressive number, but when asked which would be the best, Chioccioli keeps his cool. We are in Tuscany and we have a fantastic vine which is Sangiovese, which flourishes throughout the central part of the region and produces – in purity – a quantity of excellent wines that accompany every type of meat at the highest level. Other stories, other vines – let's forget about them, a whole book would not be enough to want to talk about them. Of course, there are exceptions and on the coast Cabernet Sauvignon and Merlot have created two indeed exceptional wines. But they are so famous that talking about them is a bit obvious. It is more fun to go in search of the right wine, knowing that when you meet a wine you like it is a personal achievement, a small joy.

Nature is strength, energy: it transforms things – in this case the pressed grapes – following a tumultuous and unstoppable process of change during which wine exists only for a very short period, an instant. Man has to govern that instant: intuit it, understand it, expand it over the years. Wonder.

> "But I believe that great happiness awaits those men
> who are born where good wines are to be found."
>
> Leonardo da Vinci

Sunset at Badia a Passignano.

A serious talk about the present and the future

Somehow so far we have talked about the past. And that's fine in the sense that the past is history, tradition, identity. But it is not to say that everything that is "past" is also good and genuine, just as it remains to be proved that everything that is modern is corrupt and soulless. We need to examine clearly – even at table or at the market – the matters that concern us closely, to avoid flawed ideological conflicts that do not help us understand reality.

The vision is that between intensive production (North American model) and extensive production (South American model) there exists a third way, which is the European one (and in particular the Italian one) which is a type of "elastic" production that adapts to the particular features of animals, of the land and which has as its primary objective the production of quality, the only way to gain by one's work.

Our diversity and the pride of being different and stubbornly wanting to stay different, is our true wealth: cultural, linguistic, human.

This whole supply chain is guaranteed by an efficient structure of control that oversees the application of the regulations and specifications of production, drafted to protect the product and the consumer, and therefore the community. From feed to animal health and welfare, from slaughtering to techniques of processing and conservation, it seeks to strike a balance between tradition and technology and maintaining this balance is healthy and beautiful. Not only that: the ties with the past, the renewal of tradition will be perpetuated only if borne forward by the passion of those who do this work as breeder, butcher, norcino or salumaio. And passion is always the bearer of quality.

In these pages we have proudly praised Tuscany, but the discourse could be extended to the whole of Italy, which at least for the quality of the food, even under a thousand different bell towers, creates a splendid national identity. Our diversity and the pride of being different and stubbornly wanting to remain so, is our true wealth: cultural, linguistic, human. It is not for nothing that we are the inventors and happy practitioners of the "Mediterranean diet", which is a simple and sustainable model that is good for everyone: people, the environment, animals. And for once we can also argue that the Italian production chain is an excellence that has served as a model for raising the quality standards of the whole European Union.

For these reasons it is essential to keep informed and be critical, especially on issues that have economic and ethical implications and that have heavy repercussions on the environment and our lifestyle. The important thing is to obtain information from reliable, authoritative sources. Behind a spectacular and incredible news story there is always someone who is trying to profit by it. Let's not trust the first bischero (a dialect term that suits the concept) who posts an opinion on internet. We should listen to those who put their name and face to their opinions.

A warm embrace to all Italians, who are all differently Italians, fond of this wonderful land in the midst of the most beautiful sea in the world.

Fr. Antonio, manager of the farm estate of the Abbey of Monte Oliveto Maggiore.

Acknowledgements

In addition to the irreplaceable help of Stefano Bancistà Falorni, I would like to thank everyone who contributed to the creation of this book:

Paolo Bacciotti, Trattoria Da Tullio a Montebeni - Coltelleria Berti Scarperia - Luca Cai e Alessandro Caldini, Trattoria il Magazzino - Giuseppe Camozzi - Trattoria La Casalinga - Cffm Montespertoli - Stefano Chioccioli - Alessandro Della Tommasina, Enoteca Pinchiorri - Vincenzo Dilorenzo, ristorante Regina Bistecca - Bar Divino Badia a Passignano - Il Norcino Roberto Falai - Daniele Falciani, ristorante Antica Scuderia, Badia a Passignano - Silvio "Gipo" Falugiani - Il Forno di Montegemoli - Paolo Gori, trattoria Da Burde - Stefano Governi - Ilenia Innocenti, ristorante il Portico - Mirko Improta e Domenico Russo del ristorante La Botte di Bacco, Radda in Chianti - Scuola di cucina In Tavola - Prof.ssa Maura Lanini - Mario Mariani - Marco Montecchi - Emanuele Parrini - Gastronomia Perini Mercato Centrale - Pierpaolo e Sergio Pollini trippai di via dè Macci - Paolo Pellegrini - Laura Peri - Roberta Perugini - Enrico Ricci - Stefano e Mino Rossi - Annette Rübesamen - Saladini Coltelli Scarperia - Agriturismo Selva di Frena, Firenzuola - Paola Senesi - Studio Santo Spirito - Daniela e Stefano Tesi - Fattoria Trequanda - Caterina Vienni, Ristorante Giovanni da Verrazzano - Beppe Zani - Angelo "Giangio" Zani, Stefano Frassineti, Trattoria "Toscani da Sempre", Pontassieve.

View of the countryside from the walls of Civitella Marittima.

© SIME BOOKS

Texts and photos
Guido Cozzi
Translation
Richard Sadleir
Illustrations
Monica Parussolo
Design
Italo Meneghini
Layout
Francesco Spagnol
Pre-press
Fabio Mascanzoni

All images were taken by Guido Cozzi except for:
p. 170 Massimo Borchi

Photos available on www.simephoto.com

First Edition 2021

CO-Publisher:
SIME SRL
ISBN 978-88-31403-07-8
www.simebooks.com
info@simebooks.com
T. (+39) 0438 402581

TETHYS BOOKS
by Atlantide Phototravel s.r.l.
ISBN 978-88-904305-3-4
www.tethysgallery.com
info@tethysgallery.com

Distribuition:
ITALY
da ATIESSE Rappresentanze
customerservice@simebooks.com - T. (+39) 091 6143954

UNITED STATES
SUNSET & VENICE, LLC
www.sunsetandvenice.com - T. 323 223 2666